HOW I BECAME A NOMADIC WORKER

a topical autobiography by Chris Lorensson

First printing in 2016. This 1st edition published 2016 by Nomadic Working

Nomadic Working is an imprint of Upptäcka Press

1918 Constitution Ave,
Fort Collins, CO 80526, USA

nomadicworking.com
@nomadicworking
nomadicworking@gmail.com

ISBN 978-0-9571428-9-3

Nomadic Working is a conscious lifestyle that uses *strategic optimization* and *experimentation* to craft a *whole, adventurous, productive* and *inspired* journey of working without an office.

Dedicated to the community of digital nomads
who have selflessly supported me.

It would not exist without Graham Spiller for his very useful mind during editing, the loving patience of my wife Ruth, the creative inspiration always available in The Rocky Mountains and the lovely folks who maintain it, and finally the loving patience of everyone I worked with in Bristol whose support proved irreplaceable.

CONTENTS

INTRODUCTION

This is the story of how I became a nomadic worker. My name is Chris Lorensson, and at the time of writing I am 34 years old, living in Fort Collins, Colorado with my wife Ruth, son Titus (5) and daughter Penny (2).

Ruth and I are busy settling down in Colorado after moving from Bristol, England, where most of this story takes place. But I grew up in Southern California, which is where the story begins.

This is an autobiography of my life as it relates to nomadic working. It isn't a *how-to* book, even though there's plenty of detailed information to be found on the topic of nomadic working.

Rather, it is a very personal record of my lifestyle, family, friends and work—and how nomadic working wove through it all during my 7 years in England and afterwards.

I move quickly through stories that are given to provide context, and then slow down into finer details where it more closely concerns nomadic working. It's an easy-read with plenty of fun and a quick pace, whether or not you're personally interested in nomadic working. So if this was a gift, sorry. But don't worry— you'll be fine.

I start at the very beginning because you should understand at least a snapshot of the circumstances which shaped me into the person I was when becoming a nomadic worker.

I have of course left out many details which I determined to be irrelevant, such as driving mom's minivan through her garage door or being chased by a possum into my own garage late one night. In fact, none of these stories involve garages (or their doors). Whether or not there are possums is a topic for another day.

My hope for this book is that you will journey with me through the adventure, love and laughter as I become a nomadic worker so that you can visualize your own journey in your mind... whether you're just *kinda interested* or already a seasoned practitioner.

I held back no emotion, shame or silliness as I wrote it, nor are facts embellished where it matters—I want you to see the story for what it is, have a laugh along the way, and take from it everything you can to become a more successful nomadic worker.

Before we begin, let's get familiar with the light at the end of the tunnel. Nomadic working is so many things, but for the purposes of right now, you should see it as nothing more than *the simple and thoughtful re-alignment of existing areas of life in order to effect a new outcome that is better in every way.* That has remained true for me.

Remember – *no new things* – only things you already know. You got this.

Starting a little over ten years ago, I've not had an office from which to do my digital design work, for the most part. I've generally explored many different places to work such as my backyard, Starbucks, local media centers, parks, nearby cities and countries. I do this because the fun experience of travel and culture inspires my work and my life, and because choosing to have fun is never difficult.

But even with proverbial travel, to do it successfully you have to identify and address the challenges that come along with it. When you travel, you pack a bag before leaving home. Nomadic working is just another vacation that requires it's own special way of packing.

Just like returning home from a trip to The Bahamas, everything you've experienced and learned by nomadic working stays with you. So the next time you pack, it's easier. After a couple times it's second-nature, and you never lose the experience or what you've learned – it just keeps building up into a huge resource – kinda like the best rollover minutes ever.

It makes me so deeply happy that you've decided to explore the lifestyle of nomadic working. From the bottom of my heart, thank you for blazing this new trail with me.

Together we can exemplify the adventurous, whole and inspired life that nomadic working offers to others in need of change. I can't wait to see what our futures hold.

Now let's start with the beginning. This is how I became a nomadic worker.

With love,
Chris Lorensson

SMALL
BEGINNINGS

I was born in Southern California in 1981 to a young couple whose relationship was already in the all-too-common throes of youthful unions, and to a big sister by 14 months; Shannon.

My parents separated before I was a year old, and my mother relocated us to the "High Desert" in Southern California because "Shannon needed cleaner air".

No—wait a second. I should start with my mother, to whom I owe perhaps the most gratitude because her impact upon my life was such that none of what follows would have happened otherwise. Her influence upon my life paved the path of nomadic working far ahead of me, as you'll see.

MY MOTHER

Robbi Ann grew up as the eldest of five; with three younger sisters and a brother in Lake Elsinore, California. It was a largely typical Californian upbringing including walks on the beaches of Orange County, sneaking out to the movies after bedtime, surfing and skiing.

Like many upper-middle-class households in the 60's on the heels of feminism and microwavable TV dinners, Robbi and her siblings grew up in a home whose mother was striving for perfection in home and family life.

But when family relationships grew difficult and unfortunate events transpired, she was put into the position of sole caretaker of her siblings in her mid-teens, with no adults remaining in the home.

Mom did what most eldest siblings would have done; she bargained with neighbors to secure rides to school for her sisters and brother, took multiple jobs to keep things running and basically became the mother of her siblings for a few years... leaving her own childhood cut short.

In such a desperate situation, she had been forced to learn how to bend the rules in order to supply the needs of both herself and her new dependents, and how to compromise in an unforgiving world.

Much of her life would become a series of occasions in which she learned to swim by being thrown into the deep end.

The incredible thing is that not only did she learn to swim, but she fought so hard that in most areas she would become the proverbial equivalent of Michael Phelps. She became a capable survivor with an uncanny ability to make lemonade when life handed her lemons.

As mom reached adulthood most of her siblings were growing up and had arranged something for themselves, which is about the time she had met my father, my sister and I were born, and then mom & dad separated. So this is where I'll pickup the story.

WESTWOOD DRIVE

We moved into a small house in Victorville, California – a smallish city just South of Big Bear Mountain and North of Death Valley – hence the name *High Desert*. I was barely 2 and my big sister Shannon was 3. Mom worked as a waitress at nights and as a nurse at the hospital during the day.

Shannon and I were so young that neither of us remember much of those days. Mom said we were with babysitters a lot (one of whom I remember crushing on). We were too young for school. For all we know we'd been trained for the circus.

But probably not, and after a couple years of settling into our new town, mom quit her jobs to start a daycare business, which is the environment in which I remember growing up.

She bought the first house in a new development on the other side of the block which she would keep for the next 15 years. Most of my childhood memories happened within those walls of our home on Westwood Drive.

I remember Christmas mornings with the tree superbly decorated in the living room, right in front of the window. I remember my birthday parties doubling as Halloween parties for everyone. I remember riding my BMX through the desert fields behind the house. I remember getting beat up around the corner with the aid of a mailbox and, at another time, beating up someone else with my He-Man lunchbox. (If you're old enough to recall, both lunchboxes and mailboxes were metal back then!) Ouch.

Mom's knack for improvisation and running a business had dramatically improved our lifestyle since before I could remember (or while training for the circus). It was easy to write off a daycare business as "not a real job", but if you had seen the caliber of operation she had setup, well… it makes me think she might have been just as effective at running some large corporation.

The garage had been entirely converted into the main playroom; complete with finished, insulated and decorated walls like the set of Mr. Roger's Neighborhood. This playroom had a half-height wall before the garage with a gate in the middle for the "clients" to enter and exit, a central HVAC system and enough toys to make FAO Schwartz look like a budding collector.

Once a year was The Great Annual Toy Cleaning, which lasted several days and consisted of every available adult hand to take shifts in disinfecting each children's book, Duplo block, Little Tikes playhouse or push-car.

The whole house was completely child-proof; every electrical socket had a cover on it, every tall object was somehow strapped down. Emergency kits were routinely checked and re-stocked, and every employee had an up-to-date police background check, Child Safety and CPR Certificate.

Earthquake kits had been assembled and were kept in waterproof rubber containers in front of the playroom's wall beside the garage door. Along with the emergency kits, they were checked and restocked twice a year, with changes noted and signed on the dedicated clipboards.

Mealtimes were more efficient than I ever remember at school, and featured far higher quality food. All day long the children enjoyed games for learning, games for singing, games for exercising, and then more games for learning. The constant games were only broken by mealtimes, snack times, nap times and the occasional birthday party or field trip or other special event.

A frequent special event would be the local Fire Department bringing a firetruck to the house, giving demonstrations of equipment and dressing up children in fire gear. After a few instances of this particular special event, the parents started showing up to take pictures. I don't know how the children kept up with mom.

Or maybe that was the plan all along.

Every year the backyard fence was taken down so that a dump truck could deliver a few new metric tons of "clean sand" into the sandbox. I never did figure out where last year's sand had gone, and could only assume it was vanishing grain-by-grain inside children's ears, hair, diapers and digestive systems. Every 2 years the entire set of swings, slides, see-saws, climbing rigs and clubhouses were replaced with new-and-improved units.

Even while keeping this finely-tuned machine operating smoothly, mom somehow managed to find time for Mary Kay makeup parties, Princess House crystal parties, Christmas parties, kids' swimming lessons, vacations to the river for boating and to the mountains for skiing with Shannon and I, and baking goods as both our classrooms' "home mothers".

Considering the situation, it would have been perfectly acceptable if the house was left in shambles after a day of 35 children running amok, but I don't recall that happening even once. The entire house was spotless after the last child was collected each day, when mom would dismiss her employees to begin cooking dinner for Shannon and I.

We had roast beef with mixed grilled vegetables one night. Another night would be the most spectacular homemade lasagna you've ever had, for which she appeared almost apologetic. Of course we didn't know the difference, and it didn't matter as long as we "mind our manners".

Every evening around the table was a formal lesson in the proprieties of fine dining. By the age of five I could have shown up at Buckingham Palace and eaten a 4-course meal across from The Queen without anyone batting an eye. Yes, really.

I remember making trips to department stores just before the start of each school year. This was a day-long outing to buy a new wardrobe and school supplies for the coming year. A day or two later the same would happen for myself or Shannon.

My clothes never had holes in them and they always looked new. Mom had always made sure Shannon and I were the most impeccably presented children regardless of occasion. This is what

I came to understand childhood to be, and I naturally assumed everyone else's was the same.

This unusually high level of perfection crossed into so many areas of life, and was echoed from her own upbringing. From the exquisitely-mannered children to the surgical perfection of her trade, mom's ways were the manifestation of her deep personal and family values that flowed into anything with which she engaged, and then maintained with what appeared to be quite an effortless grace.

She was simply re-enacting the best parts of her own upbringing – as parents tend to do – but with her own flavor of particularity. Sometimes when I visited a friend's house, I thought *how do people live like this? Are they poor?*

Just before I turned 6 my little sister Stephanie was born, and I was no longer the youngest of the family. Shannon and I were always at each other's throats those days. She was busy doing things with her friends that seemed decades beyond anything I would ever be capable of.

She was good at dancing (electric slide anyone?), loved music and went on to be a cheerleader and volleyball player in school, and would soon become especially skilled on a snowboard. She was always taller, more athletic and more likable than I was, and people naturally gravitated toward her.

She liked *New Kids on the Block* while I was still enjoying *Phil Collins* and *George Michael* along with mom. To me back then, Shannon was the definition of cool.

In those early days I was kind of a joker. I loved to make people laugh—especially Shannon. I think it was my best way to get attention during a time in which she had more important things to do.

My sense of humor carried me through many things back then. I loved watching Jim Carrey films, and pretty much anything with Steve Martin or Bill Murray (from whom I stole all my comedic ideas and imitations).

At this point in the story, you may find yourself saying *I thought this was a book about nomadic working?* That would be a fair comment. I did mention this was an autobiography, right?

Some circumstances leading up to now have made clear that I was raised in a somewhat privileged, upper-middle-class home by a mother who was strategic, loving and sometimes ruthlessly ambitious for the sake of her children.

What may not be quite as apparent is exactly whom I had become by growing up in this way. I was comical, but a quiet and gentle personality. I felt loved, safe and wanted for nothing in my environment. I spent my time enjoying school, organizing my marble collection and building things with Lego.

Compared to my peers I was short and skinny, not very athletic, afraid of getting physically hurt and far more comfortable around women than men. I hated getting dirty to a degree that might have been appropriate for an 8-year-old girl attending French finishing school.

With no father in the household, I was reaching an age where it really started to matter. I was wimpy and came to long for the things I assumed a father could give. Being raised by a household of female caretakers (however lovely) will do that to you.

But as I would later realize, I was and always would be "my mother's son", and would come to treasure her influence upon my life.

ORANGE COUNTY

Life continued in this way until I turned 12 with only
minor variations. A year or two previously, Shannon and I had
started visiting our father at his apartment in Riverside, California
one or two weekends per month.

Each time we went it was all fun and games; Disneyland trips, the
cinema, movies at home, swimming in the community pool, and
going to the beach or river. It was like a fantasy world that had
started to look so much better than what we'd become used to at
home with mom.

At Dad's we were rarely scolded, never prepared for school or made
to start with the proper fork. We never had more than one fork to
worry about at all, unless we walked over to the condiment bar at
Taco Bell for some reason.

I think that actually did happen once, but if I recall correctly, it was
so that Dad could use it to construct a tiny field-goal post for us to
shoot wads of straw-wrapper through, rather than preparing us to
invade Switzerland like mom was doing.

I was about to finish my 6 years in grade school before entering
junior high, and I made the decision to move in with dad and his
wife Kelli who had just bought a lovely home in Orange County. (I
always called Kelli "Mom" – she had earned that title well before I
ever moved in – but she's "Kelli" here for the sake of clarity.)

Shannon had just finished her first year in junior high alongside some of her grade-school friends. She understandably decided to stay with Mom.

During those weeks before moving in with dad, I remember feeling as though I had caused a lot of heartache for everyone involved in my decision, and I was probably right. No one likes to stand in court or talk to judges, but mom knew her way around better than most.

Moving to dad's was never about mom, it was about dad. Mom was already my hero. All I knew was that *I needed my dad*, and I didn't know or care about the rest because I was twelve.

LIFE AT
THE BEACH

I did not adjust easily to my new home in Orange County. I of course had no friends when starting school at the nearest junior high with the big kids. Those circumstances alone made the transition very difficult at that age. I struggled a lot through that first year, where everything felt foreign.

I eventually made a few friends and started slowly settling in. I was still very short and skinny for my age. (I had skipped a grade years earlier which made me a year younger than my peers. Strangely enough, this problem seemed to continue every year.)

At home, living with Dad and Kelli was at times pure fun, and other times a learning exercise. None of the habits of life at home I was used to were happening, and so I tried to acclimate to their way of doing things.

Looking back, it's a little easier to see what happened, and why it wasn't easy; Dad & Kelli had never really raised kids before, and they now had a kid who had been accustomed to basically living with Martha Stewart as a mom. My expectations had been set incredibly high (although I, of course, didn't realize this).

I was used to mom being actively engaged and encouraging in whatever extra-curricular activity I wanted to do, and (behind the scenes) I knew she would do everything necessary to afford the soccer cleats, rollerblades or other equipment that was needed. I never had to ask because she always anticipated my needs ahead of time.

Dad & Kelli were perfectly normal people who wore normal clothes and had normal jobs, whereas Mom was constantly striving for social and economical perfection. This difference manifested itself in quite practical ways:

Dad & Kelli didn't see the value in spending $100 on a pair of Nike shoes because they were in-fashion, whereas Mom would have not only encouraged it, but probably recommended it herself.

I was used to Mom *always finding a way to make it work* rather than acquiescing to practicalities and reason.

The timing of the move also played a big part; I was 12 years old and having just completed grade-school, in preparation for Junior High. At that age, the transition felt as if I was moving to Mars or something. I was scared and out of my depth. I was never that great at making friends, and all the big kids were tougher, taller, older and more athletic than I.

Another aspect was that *I didn't know anyone*. It wasn't like a bunch of my grade-school friends would be there with me as we explore this new world of Junior High. They were all back in Victorville. I had no one.

Then there was the culture. Victorville was a small-town mentality back then, but I had just moved into the middle of Orange

County—one of the worldwide birthplaces of cool. I felt out of my depth.

All of this coalesced into a bad recipe. With Dad & Kelli struggling to learn what to do with me, and me going through a huge amount of change at a difficult time in life, it just didn't work out well. We still had plenty of fun and good memories, but overall, I think we all felt like it was difficult.

I wasn't sure exactly what I was looking for when I decided to live with Dad, but it didn't seem like it was happening.

Looking back now as a parent myself – it's amazing things weren't worse – which I now attribute to the loving patience of Dad & Kelli.

Eventually in my sophomore year in high school I got a part-time job after school frying chicken and baking cookies at the local K-Mart Cafe. As the years went on my grades went from an annual series of straight A's at mom's to a downward spiral ending in C's and D's. In high school I was feeling depressed and had become lonely and felt misunderstood, but my friendships at school were growing stronger.

In high school I had picked up skating, which became my way of relieving the stress of home life. (When I say skating I'm referring to both rollerblading and skateboarding. I did both.) Skating become my entire world, and helped make some friends at school and at church.

I joined a "skate crew" in high school called The Dingo Squad.

As a skate crew, this meant that we would pile up into Greg's VW Vanagon and hit up local skate spots among other local outings. Most sessions consisted of me skating the entire time while the others mixed skating in-between smoking a number of different things and drinking beer.

They became my surrogate family.

Finally I was in with a popular crowd of guys I loved, and having a slice of life in which to do something I enjoyed. Things were looking up, but my grades weren't improving. The end of my sophomore year was the first happy ending I'd experienced in what felt like a long time.

Just as I had begun carving out a more comfortable niche, Shannon moved in at the start of my junior year. This represented both a welcome change with the addition of a 'friend' in the house while also resulting in the rug being pulled out from under my feet at school.

I had just built a group of friends and painstakingly crafted a reputation over the last 4 years, and with the arrival of Shannon's likable personality, I once again became "Shannon's brother" before the end of the school year, and lived in her shadow for one last time.

She started dating one of my rollerblader friends which bugged me at the time, but they eventually married and now Justin is my accomplice in crime at family gatherings.

Nevertheless, Shannon and I grew very close again during those years, and because of that it's a time that I cherish dearly. Making her laugh once again became a favorite part of my life, regardless of how often she stole my thunder in some way. She was the first to have a job, her own car, do a trip on her own and enjoyed what felt like a lot more "rope" than I ever had at dad's.

I believed others saw her as *the golden child who could do no wrong*, but strangely, the only thing about it that bothered me was the way it contrasted upon myself, and I started feeling a little less confident again. I never felt the inclination to hold her responsible for inadvertently being a little too awesome because, well, I just loved her so much, and she was just being herself.

As those high school years went by, family life at home seemed to increase in difficulty for me, which was probably just following my age. Tensions could feel very high in the house at times, and my teenager's mind let depression sneak in.

But again, looking back I realize it was all circumstantial, and nothing could have been done better by anyone. At the time I squarely blamed my father, but no one was really at-fault.

My father and I had completely opposite personalities and ways of communicating, which resulted in lots of miscommunication and misunderstanding—an unfortunate circumstance that Dad and I now recognize and even laugh about.

The fact that I was *a younger version of my mother but with less patience and wisdom* did nothing to improve the situation. But when you're a teenager it's hard to see anything clearly, let alone your own faults. I considered myself a helpless victim and that, to me, justified my actions.

But there was another side of the coin that haunted me in the best way as I lived with my father.

What Dad seemed to lack in compatibility with my personality, he amply made up for in unveiled love. With me being a classic utilitarian like my mother, this wasn't always easily received or understood, and probably never felt returned. Either way, for the first time in my life I saw what it meant to hold nothing back from people who are dear to you.

He continued to exemplify other qualities that were foreign to me; uncommonly warm hospitality, a deep love of family and a genuinely intuitive care for those around him. To me these traits were entirely new ideas, and I continued to watch in awe as my father consistently demonstrated them.

Dad's ways didn't fit into my understanding of the world that had been painted by my mother; here was love and compassion with no catch, no fallback in which he might retreat, and nothing held back.

From my point-of-view he just stuck his neck out like this all the time, and his love was so demonstrated in his actions and words that, often times, I didn't even know how to respond to it. That's kinda how I saw it; *sticking out his neck*. It was like living with a six-foot Fozzy Bear who loved Monty-Python and Mariah Carey. (Yes, he's that cuddly.)

I don't want to paint a picture that my mother is some cold-hearted diplomat who never hugged me or something, but just that her way of showing love was more reserved and utilitarian, and that was the way I was raised, and therefore what I was used to.

It made sense to me because it's exactly what I would have done. I never felt unloved by my mother, in fact, I felt incredibly loved—it was just expressed in different ways. Ways in which I understood.

Those good things I saw demonstrated by my father made residence in a corner of my mind, hanging in the balance of my 'journey into self' for years to come, and eventually shaping me in a very tangible way.

These foreign-but-lovely qualities drew people in. My father was so easy to love because he always gave more than he had and never asked for anything in-return. I didn't even remotely understand it, but I knew it was a quality I wanted in my own life, and I determined to gain it somehow.

THE START
OF NOTATION

During those days in high school I began writing poetry after having been inspired by a school assignment. The free and creative nature of it coupled with my love for words seemed to be exactly the creative outlet I needed. I wrote on napkins, cafeteria tray papers and on homework assignments.

I didn't get very far before realizing this disorganization was becoming frustrating when I wanted to go back over an old poem, but couldn't find it. I must have written hundreds of poems by the end of my sophomore year in high school. Most of which are long lost now.

Here's one of my favorite poems I've kept, just for funsies.

Brilliant after ten-or-so years Yellow Chair
holding your polished-rust-dotted arms in the air
you solemnly swear to keep them up there.
That's why I like you, Yellow Chair.

Elegance and style are so overrated
when classic design will seat one in graces
like you, Yellow Chair, do offer your patients...
comfort is latent with you, Yellow Chair.

Textiles woo over you and your use
in wondering whether to love or abuse.
Your yellowness bellows its upcoming news
of decorative sense versus years of misuse.

But I only ever use you, Yellow Chair.
(unless I need comfort to loosen my legs
or when fanciness befits a time to save face
or when we need a chair for those partying days.)

I guess your nostalgia's not in flow-y lines;
nor in pricey leather or modern designs.
Your honor is found in serving your time
by lifting your arms and getting us by.

To organize my poems, I gathered a few dollars and went to the local office supply store to begin searching for some physical method of maintaining a dedicated paper system. I settled on a 1/2" thick black 3-ring binder designed to accommodate 5.5" wide by 8.5" tall sheets. I bought two extra paper refills.

Upon arriving home I tore off all the packaging and inserted a stack of 50 pages into the binder.

I was proud at my basic-but-effective DIY. My needs were then suited perfectly, and by the end of that year I upgraded to tabbed card dividers to separate the new sections of blank and grid-lined sheets, illustrations and other things, along with a clear plastic pocket dedicated to additional pens, pencils and a clear plastic 6" ruler.

My binder became my personal information center, and I would carry it with me for the next 9 years while it evolved along with my changing needs.

I used it for journaling, which I had recently started doing. I was illustrating a lot more, and in time I even developed a little system of archiving old illustrations, journal entries, poems and notes into the divided sections at the back.

I became obsessed with being organized, and my binder had become the most useful way of exercising that obsession. I enjoyed it. I didn't realize it then, but I had become a *stationery junkie*.

I kept it mostly private and hidden from sight at all times—its contents represented the only physical manifestation of all that was in my heart and on my mind. It would also become the experience that led me to organize my notes for nomadic working. I still have this binder today.

High school is about the time my mind really started to wander. I had just been introduced to the Bible by my grandfather, and it immediately brought deep questions to my mind. On top of that, I was beginning to consider the *why* about pretty much everything.

I thought deeply about my family life, things in my Bible, and even the more philosophical sub-plots of English homework assignments. I began to feel as though I might burst. My only release for these thoughts at the time was my poetry.

I learned that most people were not interested in the things that were in my head. After a few times of trying to discuss them with friends or family, it occurred to me that the only good coming from conversing about it was that it helped me process my own thoughts.

It was a rare occurrence indeed if I received any conversational engagement—let alone a useful reply. I learned that these things had to remain my own, probably never to be shared, and I operated under that assumption for years to come.

But let me talk about journaling for a minute.

JOURNALING

Without ever thinking *I should start a journal,* I remember opening my notebook and just starting to write. I had just finished a school day and, like many other days, had met my friends at "The Steps" for some skating.

(The Steps was an outdoor area on the school campus which featured several large concrete blocks and offered us a place in which to hone our skills most days. Unusually, the school never seemed to mind that our equipment was consistently damaging the area. We never thought twice about it of course.)

Instead of lacing on my rollerblades or grabbing my board, I sat down nearby with a feeling that I just *had* to get some of these thoughts out of my mind. I opened my notebook and wrote for about an hour, until the customary time came that my friends started heading home.

I'll never forget the feeling I had while writing in that first session. It felt free—like a huge dam had been opened. I left relieved and satisfied, and it would be the start of many sporadic writing sessions like that. The fact that I was journaling never entered my head.

To-date, journaling has become more to me than just a way of relieving pressure. It's a way to calm my brain before starting to work, a way of recording what's happening in my life, a way to express my spirituality and creativity, and a way to create a sort of conversation with myself about whatever is on my mind.

It helps me process the information in my head—almost as good as having a close friend with me engaging in a conversation. Unsurprisingly, my INTJ personality type is also known as *The Absent-Minded Professor*. My journeys-of-thought often took me far from reality, and that's never really stopped.

When I'm talking about nomadic working I try really hard not to be prescriptive. I think everyone goes about things in their own way, and different things work for different people. To a degree, the nature of nomadic working demands that you do it in the way that works for you; the way that is sustainable for where you're at both personally and professionally.

I've looked back at old journal entries over the years and read about my very personal struggles and triumphs. It gives me perspective to see how far I've come, which is always encouraging and sometimes inspirational. My memory is terrible, and so many things in my history would have otherwise been forgotten.

Journaling always ends up being something different to everyone, but I've never heard anyone say *"Gee, I wish I hadn't wasted all that time journaling."* Rather there's a unanimous roar of satisfaction coming from those who journal in some form, and I can't recommend it enough.

So grab a scrap piece of paper and a coffee and just let yourself go. Don't worry about being organized, and remember that you're writing to yourself. No one else will ever read this, so it doesn't have to be perfect in any way. It's simply a free-flow of what's on your heart and mind. Let it go where it will, without inhibition. Titles, chapters, bullet points and fanciful writing will come when they're needed, without being coaxed prematurely.

The only thing I'd say for one who's just beginning is to *date every entry*, no matter what.

Journaling just happens to be one of the rare areas in which I stray from my usual line and instead say to everyone *"Yes, you should start a journal."*

It doesn't matter whether you're stuck in a cubicle 40 hours a week or relaxing on a Jamaican beach all day with an iPad and a Mai-Tai. Journaling is something that everyone should do. Go ahead, I'll wait… I'll be here when you're done. Because this is a book ;-)

HOME LIFE BREAKS

It all began to culminate at the beginning of my senior year in high school. I no longer cared for anything I was learning there. My mental adventures demanded more time than I had to give. This pressure built up until, one day, I decided to simply not go to school.

I got up in the morning as usual and lied that I would be skateboarding to school that morning. I packed my binder and Bible and left any school materials at home. I skated to the local public library where I spent the day reading my Bible, taking notes, writing poems and journaling.

The hours passed so easily that day, and the topics I focused on were enough to distract me from the primal fear in the back of mind surrounding my newfound disobedience. I had never skipped school before, and my father was not one to test. I knew that the punishment for what I had done would be severe, but I felt as though I had little choice; it was either go insane or get in trouble.

I continued to go to school as normal that week. Then, late in the week I finished my last class and went to meet my girlfriend after school. We met at a local shopping area to hang out. An hour or so later, my father showed up, fuming. I wasn't sure what he was so angry about, and it hadn't occurred to me that he might have discovered that I had skipped school earlier in the week. That was probably the most embarrassing moment of my life, being collected by my father that day.

That drive home was also the most stressful moment of my life up until that point. Dad was furious, and I felt I was being subject to a serious injustice. I had always been quite an agreeable, rather passive person, but I completely lost control of myself for the first time ever during that car ride. We both said things we would later regret.

I was instructed to stay in my room until Dad returned home from work. For me, that ride was a turning point. Upon arriving home, I packed a few things into a backpack, grabbed my skateboard and said bye to Shannon as I closed the front door behind me.

I skateboarded along the bike path to Huntington Beach, where I began living on the streets with no intention of ever returning.

It might sound as if maybe I was an unruly, disagreeable child with a long history of misbehavior and perhaps caught up with the wrong crowd. I assure you, that couldn't be farther from the truth. Maybe *caught up with the wrong crowd,* but The Dingo Squad always respected my non-participation in substance abuse and loved me for who I was.

The most 'naughty' thing I had ever done in my life was to walk home from grade school instead of taking the bus like I was supposed to, and then, of course, I had skipped school for the first time only a few days before now.

I was and always had been a relatively well-behaved child. Especially when compared to my friends at the time, I probably should have been Knighted or Sainted (if that's a thing). I had, after all, been raised by my mother – the author of social perfection.

My decision to run away was not just an act of defiance, it was the simple result of an emotional break. I could no longer fulfill the emotional capacity required to continue living this way. With this decision becoming the cherry on top of my history at home, I felt as though I had solidified my position as the *black sheep of the family*—even if that sentiment was my own.

By now I had grown somewhat out of the *wimpy little girl* I was when I moved to Orange County. Skating had lessened my fear of pain a little, and while I was by no means some football-toting jock who chopped wood for fun, what I *had* become was not entirely ideal either; a typically self-absorbed teenager with an overactive brain who saw little difference between personal emancipation and the problem of world hunger, except that personal emancipation would do something useful for me.

I hadn't yet learned much of anything from my father because I had been focused squarely on myself, and deep down, I knew this wasn't good enough.

HUNTINGTON BEACH

Having never historically done much of anything on my own, I arrived in Huntington Beach with what little cash was left in my student checking account, the clothes on my back, my skateboard and a few belongings in my backpack; my Bible, a change of clothes, the notebook containing my illustrations and poetry, my cherished stainless steel mechanical pencil and the loaf of bread and jar of peanut butter I had just purchased from the local 7-11.

First of all, if you're going to squat somewhere, Orange County is a great place to do it. I imagine that people from less fortunate countries would see squatting in Huntington Beach the same as living like a king in their own land.

I didn't know this at the time, but after traveling, a bit many years later it became apparent that Southern California is generally populated by incredibly wealthy people – most of whom have no idea how wealthy they are – and even in this dark time of my life, I was one of them.

I took for granted the fact that I had not one, but *two* families who were probably worried sick about me, and who would stop at nothing to feed me, clothe me and put a roof over my head. If it had stopped there, I would have been fortunate. But it didn't. I left a home that probably costs about a million US dollars today, and my families would have fed me fresh, healthy food, and clothed me in name-brand attire and even helped me back on my feet, be it spiritually, emotionally or physically.

I had no idea how wealthy I actually was – I had been another sad product of my own environment – and even at this low point of my life, I was richer than so many others who are suffering in the world.

I don't consider myself some kind of Jason Bourne or (conversely) some homeless bum because I spent a little time on the streets, but even squatting in Beverly Hills would teach someone a thing or two, and this short time proved to be crucial in shaping the young man I was to become.

The single most important thing I learned while squatting was this: *the world is far more flexible than most believe it to be.*

In a way I internalized the very things my mother had been telling me for years, but that hadn't really sunk-in until now. Some of the most profoundly useful truths to be learned in this life are also the most simple, like *if you want to make an omelet, you've got to break some eggs.* Duh. Others required serious excavation in order to unearth.

Like so many important lessons, I had to experience it for myself to really grasp it. But at this point, I was grateful to be doing so.

SQUATTING

While in Huntington Beach I met lots of people—some were on the streets, others were simply compassionate.

Immediately upon arrival on Main Street I went to the local skate shop and bought a new skateboard, leaving my old one behind. I bought a coffee and sat at a table outside, overlooking Huntington Beach. It was dusk and I was reading my Bible when Ellie approached me.

Ellie was a drop-dead-gorgeous barista at this café. She was maybe in her early twenties. By some unknown magic, she perceived that I had been in the middle of a tough time. When she arrived at my table she said "Hi, I'm Ellie. Are you on the streets?"

I could only assume she was asking if I was homeless, because I had never heard the term *on the streets* before. After considering my situation I replied "Yes, how did you know?" Without answering, she began telling me about some acquaintances of hers whom were also 'on the streets', and that she would introduce me to them, because they could somehow be of some assistance.

It never occurred to me that I might meet anyone or receive help from anyone, let alone *need* it. My decision to leave was a purely emotional one, and I had therefore been in no state to consider the practical realities of my new situation.

I returned an hour later, as arranged, and Ellie introduced me to John, Sarah and Dirk. John was a self-proclaimed "ex-professional skateboarder" who was short and stalky and carrying his board, but otherwise appearing completely normal in his early thirties.

Sarah and Dirk were a couple who had hitchhiked from Portland to "see the world", and were in their mid-twenties. John, Sarah and Dirk were some of the kindest people I'd ever met, but I quickly knew that John and I were going to become good friends.

That night, Sarah and Dirk left John and I to chat on the brick walls of the Huntington Beach boardwalk, on the south side of the pier. We watched the people go by as we shared our lives and circumstances. We talked about God, family and skateboarding for what seemed like hours. John had to meet some friends at a party and said we should meet up tomorrow to skate a little, so we arranged a time and place before he left.

It was dark and getting late, and I was exhausted. I hadn't thought about anything ahead of time. I spread some peanut butter on a slice of bread and thought about where I could sleep. Still sitting on the brick wall before the boardwalk, I looked around and came up with nothing after 30 minutes. I didn't really know where to begin.

After some walking around in deep thought, I returned to the pier and locked myself into a cinder-block bathroom stall the first night, right on the boardwalk. It was the only place I could find to sleep safely, since the door locked from the inside.

The gravity of my situation hadn't really dawned on me. I had never before worried about whether or not I would be able to eat or have a roof over my head. I never had to think about 'tomorrow'. Looking back, I realize that the familiarity of Huntington Beach combined with my lack of hard experiences gave me an inappropriate sense of calm, but I was never prone to panic anyway.

I was freezing on the concrete bathroom floor and sleep was difficult, but I eventually nodded off while clutching my backpack and pulling my hood over my head. Around 3 or 4am, what I perceived to be a maintenance crew started banging on the door.

It woke me up with a shock and I didn't know what to do. Scared out of my wits, I froze in panic. Should I open the door? Is it a cleaning crew or a gang of violent thugs? This world was very different indeed. I waited it out and the knocking went away.

Time passed and I had gotten to know John better, and we became good friends. I saw Sarah and Dirk several more times. Before my second night they invited to me to squat with them in the backyard shed of an abandoned home.

Inside the shed was a mess of dirty blankets and miscellaneous personal belongings pushed against the walls on the floor. At night in the shed, John, Sarah and Dirk would shoot heroin and talk about life and laugh a lot. Other nights one or more of them would never come to the shed at all.

I was happy to be, for the first time in my life, truly exploring a new experience of my choosing. It was exactly what I needed—freedom. Every now and then the thoughts of what must be happening at home worried me. I worried that police might have me on their radar, or that my face might show up on a milk carton.

These thoughts left me unsettled, but I didn't know what to do about them. I felt as though, in a way, going back home was the wrong decision, and my new taste of adventure was too strong to just give it up so easily.

Of course, as a teenager I also felt as though I had something to prove—that *I could do just fine on my own, without someone else running my life.* I felt desperate to write my own story.

Once I stopped thinking about what my family was doing, I began to look inward. I had quickly gained a new perspective on life that was so different from anything I'd experienced before, and it left me a lot to process. But now, I found myself spending most of my day on the beach reading my Bible and writing my thoughts into my notebook. I started seeing my time with John as a distraction and took more time in solitude.

I had begun a journey of self-examination that wouldn't let up for 12 years. I thought about things I had done wrong, or times I had lied. I thought about how I treated people, and how I wanted to be treated.

I thought about all the principles I was reading in my Bible, and I tried to compare them to my own history, to see whether I was a good person or not.

I developed a habit of analyzing everything I said and did. I thought about the qualities in others whom I admired, and tried to work them into my own way of living. I knew that I wanted to change, so this *exploration of self* was my way of making that happen.

Having been emancipated from the 'tyranny of parents', I gained a deep sense of responsibility for my own livelihood. I learned how influential I could be in the lives of others, and that increased my new sense of responsibility. The kindness shown by those I met on the streets reminded me of my father, and the improvisation required to survive in this way reminded me of my mother. I was shocked at how quickly this improvisation became second-nature to me.

And so, from a self-centered teenager I became a teenager with a far wider perspective on life, and a deep desire to become a better human for the sake of both myself and those around me. This was the first time I really understood that *other people had real value, and that I, too could become a person with real value.*

For the first time ever, I was in control of my own life, and felt a strong responsibility to make something of it in the best way I could.

This created the mindset I would need to start nomadic working. Doing anything differently requires a measure of self-confidence, but nomadic working requires more; a willingness to fail, an obstinance to overcome and a need for the inspiration that adventure always creates.

After that first day I never saw Ellie again, and to this day I think she must have been an angel.

BACK IN VICTORVILLE

I had found a way forward, and my time in Huntington Beach felt as though it should end. I called my mother and asked her to pick me up. I moved back into the familiar house in which I was raised, and it felt right.

My little sister Stephanie had moved out, which left only mom and I in the house that used to feel like Victorville Central Station, but had now become a much-needed sanctuary.

I got a job making coffee and mom started a music & clothing store. I eventually worked there with her, covering the odd shift, designing t-shirts and arranging "shows" with musical guests as we began planning how I would finish earning my high school diploma.

We tried homeschooling and a typical brick-and-mortar high school—neither of which were able to gain my interest enough to pull me away from my newfound mental adventures. I left both, never to earn my high school diploma.

I preferred to spend my time going deeper into my self-exploration, and found myself diving into art and music. The importance of skating began to fade away as I found more meaning in these new creative things.

Having the house to ourselves, mom and I got along famously. We watched reruns of Star Trek together, ate spaghetti and talked about life and "The Shop" we were running. We grew closer than ever, and like those last several months with Shannon, it became a time I would cherish.

Mom was exactly what I needed at just the right time—a patient and understanding "roommate" who was challenging me as much as she was willing to listen. She met me on the level I needed, and it was then that I realized how alike we really were.

A year went by in this way. I skated, wrote journal entries and poetry, worked at the store and listened to music. I made lots of new friends and spent time with them making music, watching movies and thinking more deeply about modern art. I started taking hiking trips off the nearby entry onto The Pacific Crest Trail, and that solidified my love for the outdoors. Mom and I brainstormed different ideas for The Shop and executed them together.

Being awhile into my journey of becoming a better human, I had gained a more practical perspective of the world around me. I was earning my own money and maintaining my first car. I quickly met a great group of friends through The Shop and was really enjoying this simple-but-rich life when I finally turned 18.

I began playing around more in Photoshop, scanning my illustrations or designing shirts for The Shop, among other fun things like (my own) record album covers and band logos for the music I was making at the time.

During these years I took trips back to Orange County and Los Angeles—often voluntarily squatting alone or with a friend. Since I had money, this was little more than just sleeping outdoors and mingling with those on the streets. It became a way for me to stay grounded and keep perspective.

BECOMING
A DESIGNER

One day while I was working at The Shop a friend of mom's came in and said "Hey you're Chris right? Remember that coffee mug you designed for a friend of your mother's? Well that's me. I started a company and we need a designer. Would you like to come work for us?"

I had never thought that a dropout-vagrant like myself might ever "become a designer". *Didn't he know who I was?* I had enjoyed art and illustration for years, but dabbling in Photoshop on an ancient PC does hardly a designer make. I gratefully accepted despite having little knowledge of the post. What could possibly go wrong?

(It's worth mentioning here that I'm always tempted to look back at this and think *that's not how you become a designer! You're supposed to go to school and blah blah blah...*

Actually, after more than 15 years in this field, I've learned this is *exactly* how you become a designer. It's who you know, it's being in the right place at the right time, and it's having work that speaks louder than a certificate. Nothing wrong with school, it just wasn't for me.)

The next week I became the first and only designer for the largest charter school organization in the Pacific Southwest, making

$30,000 a year, which was about $29,000 more than I knew what to do with.

I remember all this money going into my checking account for the first year and just piling up. All of my needs had been satisfied already when I was just making coffee or selling t-shirts, but I tried to eat out more.

I visited second-hand stores more frequently (my clothing shops of choice), but never really made a dent in it, so I just started paying for everything whenever I went out with friends.

I was eventually transferred into the Business Development Department which was managed by my mom's friend, and our job there was to create companies and see if they made money. If they didn't, we scrapped them. If they did, we decided what else to do with them.

One such company was a small indy record label which eventually grew into its own building, started its own clothing line and music magazine while launching new bands. Along with a few others from the department, I permanently moved over to the music label's building.

In almost everything I was learning-by-doing. If we needed a website, I learned how to make a website. If we needed a marketing strategy, I learned how to do it. The list went on and I was learning at a rate that no design school could have ever maintained.

Of course, I made lots of mistakes along the way, but as the sole person in charge of anything related to design, my sense of responsibility and love for learning got me through while having lots of fun. My now heavily-stroked ego supplied a lot of motivation, too.

During my time at the label I created a private little avant-art group. My aim was to foster a small community of hand-selected artists (including myself of course) in order to showcase our talents online and through small art shows at various SoCal venues.

Before long a few shows eventually emerged, and in organizing those I began to get involved in the modern art scene in Los Angeles. I met a few designers, artists and gallery owners and was able to pick their brains about how they found success while simultaneously maintaining some level of personal integrity.

This little art group was expanding my horizons to the wider art community, which is the only place I could see meaningful art being done. Looking back, I realize I had been yearning for meaning in my own design work, and it led me to seek out such manifestations wherever I recognized it happening—but I never realized I was doing it.

I saw that the design world was far bigger than my little private corner, and realized so much could be done by connecting with people outside my own tiny world. This spurred to me initiate collaborations of art shows, design projects and even poetry from then on—whether formally exhibited or not. This love for collaboration only deepened after my little art group stopped.

Back at the label, I eventually hired and managed a 4-person design team to fulfill the widely varying needs of the label. I got lucky a lot (in terms of business, you dirty bird), but I had also been thrown into the deep end and, like my mother, learned to swim in that way.

By the age of 22 and with little-to-no prior experience, I learned to be a Chief Designer and then Creative Director of those two different large companies.

I worked there for almost 4 years before finding my own place and moving to The Arts Colony of Pomona, California. Over the coming years I saw the records, shirts and magazines I had designed being enjoyed out 'in the wild', and found satisfaction in the fact that something I had created was in some form, still 'alive'.

This stoked a new desire to create *lasting* things and forever changed how I looked at my work. I knew that any purely digital projects would never satisfy this desire. But right now, I had no control over which projects landed on my desk, and it began to make me feel dissatisfied.

DESIGN
IN POMONA

It was early in October of 2005. I was about to turn 26 and getting through my third year at a design agency as their Creative Director. We were designing ads, brochures, logos, websites and commercials for Cadillac, K&N, HUMMER, Toyo Tires and others in the automotive and political markets.

With this new role I focused on a larger strategy of climbing the corporate and social ladders as quickly as my experience would allow. This egotistical drive temporarily distracted me from my desire to create products that would stand the test of time.

In those days I spent a lot of my "off time" illustrating and improving my Photoshop skills. I was deep into the SoCal art scene, and getting very interested in experimental art—especially landscape and architectural art. I attended galleries and meetings in Los Angeles on both subjects. In a way, this was another manifestation of my desire to find meaning in my own work.

Inevitably, my idealism had always caused me to be critical in some way. Being in an old-school industry like design had its share of downsides. I loved designing, but I grew to loathe the industry and its practices… like being stuck inside an early Mad Men episode. Having learned what made the whole thing tick, I thought I could do it better. So I tried.

During my first 6 years in design I had tried to go freelance twice. Both times I fell flat on my face and I couldn't figure out why. Looking back, of course, it's clear as day; the experience I gained at agencies wasn't enough to run my own business—let alone running my own business in the way I wanted to.

I became deeply dissatisfied with my design job because I knew that nothing I was making would last more than a few months—such is the nature of much digital work.

I thought about how I could gain some freedom from the industry while still earning a living, but my creative tendencies never let me rest. This was a similar feeling I'd had before running away from home many years earlier.

But to get past that, let's see what it all looked like in practicality.

THE POMONA ARTS COLONY

I lived at 193 West 2nd Street (unit B) in Pomona, California in a 90-year-old brick building that used to be a hotel. It was right across the street from the famous music venue The Glass House, the crown jewel of The Pomona Arts Colony. Parts of *The Cat in the Hat* were filmed right in front of the place I rented for $650 per month.

It was almost 4,000 square feet and technically had a total of 13 rooms spread over 2.5 floors. That point-five is the loft above the kitchen, which I had made my bedroom and which was accessed by means of a wooden ladder. The ceilings of that ground floor must have been 40 feet high, but I never did measure it.

Looking back, it was probably so cheap because it should've been condemned decades earlier. It was ratty with exposed brick and very few finished walls, but I loved it. I called it *The Studio*, and as a designer, I liked being able to invite friends to "The Studio."

I had bought into the game. In the morning, I dressed as much like a designer as I could before driving toward the office in my shabby-chic 1991 Mitsubishi Montero. I sat in the café across the street before work, usually writing poetry or journal entries. I did my morning hours at work before resuming my writing at the deli over lunch. I did my afternoon hours before returning home at about 6:30 each night.

After work I would usually meet some friends to either drive to a dance club or art show somewhere in LA, or I would go downstairs to my makeshift office and work on whatever art project I was doing at the time. Weekends were spent doing much of the same, just without the office hours.

Being a 'car guy', I purchased a 2003 Infiniti G35 sedan in silver. It was my first 'nice' car. I really enjoyed looking more 'like a designer' in that car. Being just 25 years old, I had seen more success than any of my peers, and it was something that made me slightly uncomfortable and gave me a rather ugly sense of pride. I had come from a family culture and place in which success was a big deal. The true depth of that dark side of SoCal culture wouldn't become clear to me for a couple more years.

Being the black sheep of the family felt like something that was slowly fading away. I remained largely uncommunicative with most of my family—including my father. In fact, I hadn't had a real conversation with him in years. I was focused on my new ego-driven existence and enjoying it for the most part.

Life in Pomona was fine until something would remind me of how unhappy I was, deep down. I felt very little freedom, pinned down to a job that had me doing what I considered to be meaningless work in order to maintain a lifestyle that wasn't really 'me'.

But I tried hard to make it work—I was clubbing with friends and going to fancy art shows. It was as though life had chosen a path for me, and I simply accepted it without really thinking. I stuck to it for so long because I enjoyed the affirmation it brought.

That was perhaps the first time in my life where I really felt as though I had achieved something notable, because *everyone else seemed to think so.* But I had always measured my success using a different yardstick.

Eventually I was rubbing shoulders with reasonably well-known designers, going to far more important parties and schmoozing at art conferences. I'd take my car to detailer's and find new artsy knickknacks which I could then show off during my annual Swedish Christmas Party.

My ego was the only thing keeping me going, and I knew I had diverted from the path I wanted to be on. I was doing all the things that were supposed to make me happy and none of it was working. So I quit my job, renounced all material possessions, took an oath of silence and hitchhiked to Tibet.

All of that is true except that bit about Tibet. That's not what happened at all. Sorry.

FOREIGN GUESTS

I have this friend named Shön (as he preferred it at the time). He's an accomplished recording artist, and had been a close friend for many years. He was staying with me at The Studio for awhile.

Shön had been all over the world for music, and being a social butterfly, had real friends from each country in which he'd performed or recorded. It became commonplace for these international friends of his to visit and stay at The Studio.

In fact, that's how I met my first Englishman, Matt. He and I were about the same age and Shön invited him to stay at The Studio. Shön was busy recording one evening and asked me to show Matt around.

Matt and I drove to a famous little jazz club for a simple night out. We ordered a couple beers before claiming the last table situated within inches of the stage, where a sensational jazz performance was underway.

We had continued the pleasant conversation that had started on the drive over, but being so close to the stage got us in the habit of yelling our conversation across the table. With timing that couldn't have been better had it been edited in Hollywood, Matt stood up as the song hit a quiet spot and yelled *"Mate, I'm GASPING for a fag!"*

The only thing that didn't immediately stop, thankfully, was the band. (In England, *fag* means cigarette, but not here in California.) Not as embarrassed as I expected, Matt went out front for a smoke and became my second-most-memorable guest Shön ever brought home.

Now let me tell about the *first* most memorable, which followed a few months later.

RUTH

Shön had mentioned earlier in the week that one of his friends was coming to stay awhile. I think his guests had become so common an occurrence that I forgot he'd mentioned it at all.

I had been out at a club with some friends and came in around midnight after driving to Hollywood and back, dancing, and probably having too much to drink. The door opened, and I remember a chilly breeze coming in alongside Shön and his rather angelic guest, Ruth. My spirit was quickened at the sight of her.

They walked in and Shön made introductions. It was clear that everyone was done for the day. Ruth and I made chit-chat for a couple minutes, and then I showed her downstairs to her bedroom.

After returning upstairs I met Shön in the kitchen and said "You didn't tell me she was HOT!" Looking back, I don't feel that these words were an accurate representation of what I was feeling.

Months later I would learn that, despite Ruth not having shared my sentiments in that particular moment, that night she would dream of me being back home with her in England while I met the most important people in her life.

She must have awoken quite confused… but at least the universe tried to make it clear that *this was meant to be.* (Hey Universe, air-five!)

In real life I have a tendency toward understatement that winds its way through most areas, so I'll try to be more explicit here. Meeting Ruth that night had left my heart in an instant turmoil for which the only remedy was, well, *Ruth*. As others have described it, it was *love at first sight*, and I felt this deeply as the rest of the story should reveal.

I should also note that my deeper unhappiness at that time had led me to seriously consider moving to Sweden to study furniture design at Konstfack and meet the other side of the family who never emigrated to America. My heart already had both feet out the door, but the weight of my ego had thankfully held me back.

Ruth stayed with us for a total of ten days, during which I desperately tried to get time off work to spend with her. As a rather comical and unfortunate coincidence, Shön wasn't recording or touring just then and so it was hard to get time alone with Ruth and away from Shön (who always wanted to laugh and rarely be serious).

I managed to get a day off work and take her to Santa Monica beach, where we talked about everything including our mutual belief in God, what our lives had been like and about the anecdotal differences between England and California.

After that we all took a weekend trip to Las Vegas. I spent every moment I could with her while she was with us. The only other significant time I got alone with Ruth was during one of her last days with us at The Studio.

I took her for a walk around the local college campus late

that night. We sat on a cement bench and I said *"Look—I don't want to freak you out or anything, but it's important that you know I'm planning to move to England to marry you."*

You start to get an idea of my unusually high tolerance for risk, and as I prefer to put it, opportunism—not that Ruth was a risk, but leaving what I had built and the risk of her not feeling quite the same. Usually my tendency toward inappropriate transparency got me into trouble.

Time would tell on this one.

BATTLE OF THE EGO

By this time in life, having lived on my own in a grown-up world for awhile, I had become a little more mature and a little more wise. I learned how to do things I didn't want to do, like go to work, file taxes and change my engine oil.

I was gentle with people and still in the habit of constantly scrutinizing my own thoughts and actions. I continued to think about the qualities I loved in my parents, my sisters and some of my friends.

I tried to be more openly loving like my father, I tried to be more strategic like my mother, I tried to be more outgoing like my big sister, and I tried to be more opinionated like my little sister.

The constant flow of friends through my life was a river of opportunities to think about why I loved them, and then to explore and embrace those qualities in my own life.

In all of it, I never forgot who I was. I knew when I was right, and I knew when I was wrong. To me, the whole point was for me to change. I never felt a need to be fake, but the life I was living wasn't really 'me'—it was just too easy to stay in it. But my end-game was, after all, about *authenticity;* becoming a better version of who I already was.

I constantly battled my ego in those days, and it was made visible by so many contradictions;

I spent free time exploring how to be a better person and then practicing it, after which I drowned my sorrows in music, art, and dancing and drinking at clubs. I treated my friends like they were the most important thing in my life, but then relied on my ego to lead me to happiness. I was more than aware of these inconsistencies—they were constantly plaguing me.

I embraced the natural qualities I had since I was little; creativity, curiosity and a penchant for comedy, opportunism and improvisation. My time in Huntington Beach had stripped away most of my fear and inhibitions.

I loved what was happening to me as a person on the inside, but my practical situation of being a designer and living in this way needed to change. It just wasn't me and I knew it.

I believed that to be truly authentic, my lifestyle should outwardly match what was in my heart, which was *love, the need for adventure* and like most, the need for *meaning*.

PLANNING
FOR ENGLAND

Ruth returned to England and I started planning ways in
which to follow. When I turned 26 just days later, I began
my preparations by shedding as many possessions as I could.
(It's amazing what you can accumulate over years with almost
4,000 square feet!)

I handed in my notice at work, put my car on the market and
began letting my friends and family know what was going on—
that I had bought a one-way ticket to England to leave in one
month's time. From the time Ruth left The Studio to the time I
arrived in London was about 60 days.

I had both friends and family trying to talk sense into me, and for
the first time in years I remembered how I had felt like the black
sheep of the family. Knowing what this sudden decision looked like
on paper made me a little uncomfortable, but by this time I had
largely become accustomed to feeling disapproved-of by others.

In fact, I felt this so often that I became proud of how easily I
was able to shrug it off. My life as a designer had become the
façade behind which I hid with all my deep thoughts and personal
challenges. But I finally had something strong enough to overcome
the ego that was holding me back from my quest for authenticity.

I had never really traveled much before. The farthest from home I'd ever been was a short week in New York for the record label, and Encinitas, Mexico—which is basically just an extension of Southern California (but with better fish tacos and lacking any noticeable food prep standards).

I knew how little I understood of Ruth's country, so plane ticket in-hand and my flight just days away, I did what any normal person would do and Googled *england*.

After perusing online amidst flogging my belongings and finishing my last days at work, all my suspicions of England were confirmed, and I learned a few new things too;

The British really *do* have bad teeth, everyone does seem to know The Queen, and tea is a real drink with different flavors and everything! (I would later learn that it's also a snack, a full meal, two different times of day depending on who you ask, and both a question and a greeting.)

Google informed me that in England, men wear bowler hats and use canes, and the British garment industry had never imported any colored fabrics, so London looks like Manhattan in the winter – a sea of black wool – but with hats and canes to make it *more English*. I was pretty sure that The Queen, Ruth and Mrs. Doubtfire were the only British women. Ever.

And that all the men were clones of either Michael Cane, Dick Van Dyke or John Cleese. (I would later learn that Dick Van Dyke is from Missouri.) And it rains a lot. (This turned out to be the only thing I actually got right.) I had expected it to be different from what I was used to, but I was glad to be prepared for my new home country. *Thank God* for the internet. No really.

The British weather was what everyone kept talking about and I compared it to California. Contrary to popular belief, there is snow and cold weather in Southern California. Just not a lot of it.

My siblings and I had the fortune of taking ski trips in our youth, which meant that I was one of the most 'seasoned' Southern Californians I knew. With my leathery hide and encyclopedic knowledge of Great Britain, I began packing.

I threw out or gave away most of my shorts; saving only a single pair of flip-flops and my warmest boardshorts. Thankfully I had recently treated myself to a shopping spree at Banana Republic, which was all the rage in 2005. I had some very nice button-ups, a couple real-wool collared sweaters, and a few pairs of nice trousers.

(It's worth noting that the only reason to ever own a piece of wool in California is purely for the sake of fashion, because it's rarely a practical choice.)

If I recall correctly, I also packed a newish pair of black Converse All-Stars. For Southern California, that's kinda like wrapping reindeer skin around your feet and tying it off with tree roots because you're clearly preparing to scale Mount Everest in winter with some Sherpas. We don't really *do* shoes that much—at least that had been my experience.

If there's anything I learned from my parents by then, it was to *always have clean underwear.* It was to be, and I saw that it was good. I was packed and enjoying my last look around The Studio.

As a last-minute decision I grabbed my skateboard before locking the door behind me for the last time. With my ride to the airport waiting and the entirety of my belongings in a large forest green Kirkland Signature suitcase donated by my mother, I was ready to enter the unknown and 'claim my bride'.

I knew it would be okay to use that term because England was only *just* exiting The Dark Ages. As such, I knew The British would appreciate me sharing the following American inventions: fashion, skateboarding, MTV, coffee, The Beatles, toothbrushes, the wheel. This was going to be great!

WHAT. THE. HECK. BRO.

On November 3rd, 2005 I cleared customs at Heathrow Airport and stepped onto the streets of London; The land of the 49p Cornish Pasty, Indian food *you can actually eat,* and a surprising number of completely normal people.

I was shocked to not have been greeted by The Queen, but I figured she must be very busy feeding all those corgis and keeping her collection of Land Rovers running, and so I let it slide.

After all, I knew that dogs were hard work from experience, and that Land Rovers require spontaneous poetry recitations and the odd rose-petal milk bath in order to keep running.

London was as eye-opening as the first time I stepped into Times Square. I genuinely had no idea what to expect. Even the movies in my head hadn't truly prepared me for that which I was now standing right in the middle of.

Great Britain is one of the most curious and beautiful countries I've ever had the pleasure of experiencing, even after all the travel that Ruth and I would later do.

It's no wonder the strangest children's books like *Alice in Wonderland* are English—as Alice says, *"Curiouser and curiouser!"*

There's a certain magic about the place that's hard to describe.

As I exited the airport with my suitcase every sight, sound and smell was new. For the first time in my life I saw an English pub. The streets of London now had a very real quality about them which I was seeing with my own eyes, but somehow that didn't take away from the magic I had in my mind about it. I've never felt that feeling again about anywhere else.

I immediately sensed that this was not just a move, but that this was going to change everything about my entire life, forever. And all of that was starting now.

The first thing that happened according to my research was that *I met with Ruth,* who I had only seen a handful of times in my entire life (but we had spoken with on the phone every day since she'd left California).

Arriving in London and seeing Ruth is one of my happiest memories. She took me to a local English pub for my first "pub lunch" before catching a showing of *The Curse of the Were-Rabbit* at Leicester Square Theatre. We left to board the train for Bristol, which was about an hour southwest of London.

SETTLING
INTO BRISTOL

The first few days are a blur of pubs, houses and people. Ruth had just completed the purchase of the house at 7 Dalrymple Road, and was planning to rent out her flat around the corner where she had been living.

We weren't married of course, which meant that we couldn't live together. Ruth was a pastor, and living together "out of wedlock" would certainly have been frowned upon.

I attended Woodlands Church that Sunday and met a lot of people. Apparently the fact that Ruth had met "a boy from America" had been a recent hot topic in the community, because the following Monday someone walking by on the street stopped me and said *"You're Chris, right? Ruth's ummm.."*

A little surprised, I confirmed the accusation and carried on. This was to be the first of many similar encounters during the next few years.

7 Dalrymple Road was "in a state" as the British say. Nearly 200 years old, the exterior walls appeared to be supported only by the growing moss that joined them to the houses on the left and right. Aside from the 60-year-old wallpaper and lighting fixtures, and to my relief, the structure appeared largely intact from the inside—

likely fortified by the twenty-odd layers of paint.

I was convinced that the exposed floorboards made up the original foundation of the house, and were in need of attention (in 'Californian' that means *replace them immediately, burn the remains and hire a priest in hopes that it might somehow, someday, be made holy again).*

The house at Number 7 had two bedrooms, a dining room, a living room, a basement, a bathroom and a conservatory. There was a fireplace in each of those except the kitchen and adjacent conservatory (yes—there was a fireplace in the bathroom).

My substantial Googling had informed me that fireplaces were originally meant for *heat,* rather than for decoration. And so the abundance of them in the house did not inspire confidence regarding the heating situation.

I soon learned that my skepticism was warranted by the fact that the house needed a new "boiler", and would not have any heating until it had been supplied. *What the heck is a boiler?* When I asked about central heating Ruth replied *"What's that?"* We had a lot of those kinds of conversations over my first couple years there.

All of this was contrary to my own experience in which, when one becomes uncomfortable due to temperature, all one had to do was to *push that button over there.* So many daily things I would learn about in England would follow this general pattern. *No, look. Use that hand-crank. Sorry, it's steam-powered. You can't just use water—it only runs off the tears of a thousand unicorns.* That's something of the impression I got, anyway.

So I stayed at Number 7 while Ruth bunked in a spare room at her sister's house around the corner. Her old flat had been rented out.

I took a few days in England to explore a little by foot, with Ruth leading the way. She had a 1997 Peugeot 302 in cherry red in the flat's detached garage, but it probably wasn't running and she didn't have a driving license.

To this day I have no idea why I never tried to drive it myself, especially considering that I genuinely liked the sporty little car. We eventually sold that garage separately from the flat (only in England!), along with the little red Peugeot inside it.

Our transportation consisted of walking and taking the occasional city bus. We walked miles every day, literally. Ruth had been doing this for years, but the last time I had walked more than a half mile in a single session was hiking on California's Pacific Crest Trail years earlier.

I was not prepared for it, and if I were to describe Bristol's topography it might resemble the hand-motions of a musical conductor. Just on a physical level, I was being stressed to my maximum almost daily.

During my third night it snowed, and I awoke to a more serene England that was created by the collective British reluctance to do much of anything when snow falls. I showered and began rifling through my stuffed suitcase for warm clothes. I put on a pair of skin-tight jeans, a Banana Republic button-up shirt and cream-colored knit hoodie.

My feet were shod with a pair of borrowed socks inside my new black Cons. *You mean I actually need SOCKS too!? This is just crazy.* I realized I was going to need a pair of shoes that were even more robust than these, so we ventured out onto the English Tundra in search of them.

Not a soul was in sight as Ruth and I walked to the city center's shopping area Broadmead. Thankfully we both only lived a few blocks away. Not having much money, I spotted a pair of Clarks Wallaby knock-offs on sale and made the purchase, which marked my first opportunity to learn from my mistakes when preparing for English weather—and I was about to learn exactly how important those decisions would become.

We walked back to Ruth's sister's house to settle in over a fire and some tea, and I got to know Ruth's family a bit more.

The next day was my first day back to work. I had one unfinished project which I had brought with me from California. I bundled up and went downstairs to my new dining room, set up a little workstation on a makeshift table, and wearing most of my clothes and a blanket across my lap, I got to it.

The first few days of working were nice; I was still firmly in the honeymoon phase of being in a new country, and everything was exciting then.

I was also happy to be free; not having a desk job and responsible for my own time every day. Was this what I had been looking for? In a way, it was. The simple sense of adventure stimulated my mind. That was enough to keep me happy for a time.

DESIGN COMPANY

The honeymoon phase subsided and we both got back to work. I'd been working in the dining room for a month or so and began to feel that I was missing out; staring at the same four walls seemed to sap my creativity. I had run out of money and wouldn't be paid for any projects for awhile.

I needed more work and I needed to get out. This was my chance to finally get some British clients and arrange some of the practicalities of running a small business in England. After all, for the first time since I left Huntington Beach, I had nothing to lose.

I walked into town and opened a bank account in my own name, and one for the business. I went online and filed for a sole-proprietorship license and my business was born.

Word caught on at church that I was a designer, and a few small church-related projects started rolling in. I designed a flyer and website for a small group at our church among other projects.

Even though it was a far cry from directing photo shoots for Cadillac or commercials for Toyo Tires, I was happy to be out on my own without much to lose. It felt free. I signed up to a slick online billing service, made a company logo and created a website. Things were going well, and just enough money started rolling in to cover my basic expenses.

I had never run my own business before, so everything was new to me. I was aware that I needed to 'officially' file for a business license, that I wanted to get a website and brand created, and that I needed clients. Everything beyond that was a learning curve.

Eventually I experienced many various needs; the need for a proper billing system, to stay organized and keep files backed up, to maintain a list of client contact details and things like that.

Other things, however, were far less apparent, and before long I realized why I had failed my two previous attempts at going private.

As I communicated with clients on new projects, I realized that what clients *want* and what clients *need* are often two different things. I learned that clients didn't understand the language of design, and that I had to offer a far more concise, even elementary level of direction and description.

I would notice that some projects were taking far too long, and I would sit down to find the cause for the delay. The client lacked an understanding of the next step, or realized they needed more work than they had originally anticipated.

I experimented with various ways to address these problems. If a client was stuck on supplying content for their new website, I offered a free content outline in an email, alongside a paid option to have me sit down and develop the content with them.

I had experiences where a design did not match the client's expectations, and I eventually began to sit down with clients before starting any work to get more detail about what they really wanted. I learned to preempt as many of these things as I could.

But not all of it could be addressed ahead of time. I learned that no matter how detailed a project brief was, a client would always want to tweak things after-the-fact. I changed my estimates to cater for the 'free time' all clients expected. All of these things went fine as long as I would *expect the unexpected,* and then of course, consciously learn from them.

With more work on the schedule and word traveling quickly, my clients changed from church-based to the public domain of small-to-medium businesses. I was busy learning how to manage expectations, communicate clearly, write estimates and bill accurately. I knew I had finally gained enough momentum for this new business to 'stick', and that made me happy.

Another happy coincidence – and one whose significance I may never truly understand – is that I was now a big fish in a little pond. I'd spent the last 6 years actively fighting my way up the corporate ladder and schmoozing my way into important work-related relationships.

This was just *how you did things* in Los Angeles if you wanted to amount to anything. To me, it had become second-nature. But in Bristol's small-but-tighly-knit creative community, I probably appeared like some ego-centrical shark.

I started strong compared to my previous two attempts back in California. Perhaps that was because my situation had changed; my environment was entirely new, so everything around me felt like an opportunity.

At the same time, I had no fall-back option. This rendered everything a necessity. I never did look for a full-time job—for the first time in my adult life, my expenses were very low and I owned almost nothing. Just *moving* had changed my entire situation in regards to money, possessions, need and risk. I didn't need a full-time job. It felt liberating.

WORKING REMOTELY

With some spending money and lots of work on the schedule, I decided it was time to venture outside of the dining room for some fresh inspiration. The house had become a lonely place, and without a lot of money for improvements, I opted to enjoy the functional heating system at Starbucks.

Every day I walked into town and sat at the same seat, ordered the same Café Mocha, logged onto the same wifi network and saw the same baristas. I was enjoying the change of scenery and feeling the excitement of getting out of the house and into this new world.

Why Starbucks? Probably because I'm from California, and when you want to work away from the office, it's just where you go. I can remember going to Starbucks to 'work' as far back as my junior year in high school.

Ruth and I spent lots of time together between our work schedules. We also traveled more than I ever had in my life that first year; to Dublin, Barcelona, Austria, France, Wales and of course London.

I got involved in a charity she co-founded, *LoveBristol*. We dreamed together a lot at pubs, in front of fires and over beer, wine or tea. Everything about Ruth was right, and on this occasion my choice to trust my instincts had paid off.

Being "out in the wild" – whether that be the city or the wilderness – had always been preferable to me because it wasn't home. I never liked being at home for as long as I can remember;

When I was young and my mother ran her daycare business, my room was off-limits during the middle of the day and when I returned from school because it was nap-time and the kids needed to be separated. So my bedroom was occupied by one or more [snot-nosed rugrats] who were supposed to be asleep.

When I did come into the house – especially during nap time – I was usually "asked" to perform some task like washing the dishes, folding the laundry, cleaning up a mess or some similar daycare-related job.

I learned early-on that being at home meant *not* being able to have fun, and I carried that mentality with me into adulthood. Almost two decades later some colleagues would recognize this trait in me and christen it "Ricky-Bobby Syndrome", referencing the Will Ferrel film *Talladega Nights* in which the hero's transient father panics when anything starts 'going as it should'.

For me, though, it would prove a crucial personality trait that egged me on my journey of 'designing' my life and work. Once again, making lemonade.

ATLANTIC ENGAGEMENT

I had entered England on a 6-month "Visitor-VISA", which meant I was allowed to "visit" for six months before I had to head back to California. (No—I hadn't thought of this ahead of time.)

In my mind I thought *there's probably something 'official' I'm supposed to do, but I'll worry about that later. I was in California, and now I'm in England, and that's close enough for now.*

As this deadline loomed, I looked into the matter of staying in England to marry one of its residents a little more closely, at which point the British Embassy informed me that we had to obtain a special "Marriage VISA" from the British Embassy in Los Angeles.

In short order we booked an impromptu flight to LA and arranged a couple short visits with family, but focused on making sure we had collected the myriad documents to satisfy the requirements of the VISA. Little did we know that large-scale operations like this would become the norm for us if we were to remain together in England.

Whether or not I would be able to remain in England *at all* was now in question. It all depended on this VISA being granted, which felt as unpredictable as the weather outside.

We learned that the basic idea was that we had to prove that *we were indeed a real couple who was truly in love* (as opposed to maintaining a front for some terrorist act.)

In time and after years of similar situations, we became accustomed to this stance of *guilty until proven innocent,* and with the Twin Towers attack on September 11th not being too far behind, nationalist sentiments were not in our favor.

On the plane trip out, we decided that by the time we returned to England we should be officially engaged. We landed in Los Angeles and spent a little time with friends and family over our short 3-day visit. On the day, we arrived early near the embassy and dropped into a jewelry store to buy Ruth an engagement ring.

We made our appointment on-time, and much to the reticence of our British Embassy representative, I obtained the VISA I needed to return to my new home. Ruth and I were ecstatic and relieved that we would, after all, be able to continue the relationship which we had set into motion.

On the ride back to LAX for our return trip home, it occurred to me that I had not formally proposed to Ruth, and that the decision to be engaged by the time we got back home was hanging in the air. My spider senses informed me that Ruth was getting uncomfortable and perhaps even worrisome about this unfortunate oversight.

Side note: It's particularly funny to look back at that day almost a decade later with a deeper understanding of how much self-control Ruth must have exercised to remain silent!

On the plane, we chatted a little about our trip and how we were thankful that we had obtained that crucial sticker in my passport. In time, Ruth fell asleep and the unfulfilled task of proposing was now seriously nagging at me.

I was never one for "romantic moments", and that was an area in which Ruth and I were polar opposites; she loves for everything to be special in some way, and I had been slowly learning this fact as holidays, birthdays and special occasions passed.

I, however, have the sentimentality of a cardboard box.

This musing only increased my level of discomfort, and (however unrelated,) I arose to visit the restroom. On my way toward the back of the plane, a stewardess hung the intercom back on its hook opposite the bathroom door. It gave me an idea. I motioned for her attention as I approached to whisper into her ear.

The stewardess woke Ruth with the announcement that *one of our passengers has something special to share.* In a sleepy daze, Ruth looked back in shock as she found me kneeling while the stewardess passed the intercom. I fumbled for the box containing the engagement ring and struggled against the intercom's cord that had wound its way around my arm. I finally managed to grip it between my cheek and shoulder as I said something like *"Ruth, we've been dating for a long time, and I'm so stoked to know you. Will you marry me?"*

Yet again, the exact words I uttered did not in any way reveal what was in my heart, or what should probably have been written and rehearsed into a mirror during weeks prior. Despite my in-articulation, passengers began cheering as Ruth accepted my humble offer.

I returned to my seat and a few minutes of coo-ing went by before the stewardess presented us with the airline's bottle of champagne along with two clear plastic champagne flutes and a simple *congratulations*. Ruth asked me what "stoked" means.

As we stopped giggling, none other than the plane's captain himself grabbed the intercom for a long and heartfelt exposition on how *he and his wife had been married for a million years and were still so in-love*.

Then I was reminded... I got up to go to the bathroom.

Serendipity had smiled upon us and my improvisational talent proved to be a match for Ruth's romanticism. We returned to Bristol – new VISA in-hand – and officially engaged. One of us made sure the entire city knew as quickly as possible.

THE DIGITAL TIDE

In the early 2000's *remote working* was barely a term in itself, let alone it's cousin Nomadic Working. Speaking widely in the realm of business, on the unusual occasion that the business determined they had a legitimate need for an employee to permanently work somewhere other than in the office, it was called *telecommuting*, and these employees were basically expected to pretend they were in the office as best they could.

They had to answer the landline, be at their desks during the same 8 hours as the rest of the company, and be able to respond to requests and tasks in the same manner as anyone else. Working from home was bad enough—the idea of not having an office at all was unconscionable.

Sometimes, even the typical employment requirements weren't enough, and telecommuters were made to adhere to an additional company manual with an official *Procedure for Telecommuting* and submit an hourly report for each day or week. After all, the business was paying someone a wage, but they weren't sitting in the office, and this had to be not only controlled, but quantified and justified should anyone higher up ask about it.

Telecommuters were considered as probably lazy and undeserving of their unusual freedom, and were often disliked by those who were required to be in the office. It was a lose/lose on most accounts. Anything outside this reality was a genuine anomaly. But then things started to change.

Remote working became a small meme on the internet. Bloggers started trickling out a little article on the subject here and there. At more 'hip' companies, remote working was starting to carve out its little corner.

In 2009 entrepreneur Timothy Ferriss wrote a book called *The 4-Hour Work Week*. In it, Tim (probably) coins the term "The New Rich", in-reference to the new wave of workers who are quite literally working nomadically; they're leaving home for months and years on-end, and working as they do so – sometimes they're leaving the entire concept of 'home' behind.

Though Tim's book is largely focused on hacking the system of work and life, his open-mindedness to different methods of working was one of the first times this idea really made it out into the public on a high-profile scale, with tangible examples and results to back it up.

In October 2010 Jason Fried of Basecamp gave the TED Talk *Why work doesn't happen at work*, and it was like the dam was breaking. Then in 2013 Jason and David Heinemeir Hansson wrote a book called *Remote*. Basecamp (then 37SIGNALS) had been pioneering and promoting the ideas of remote working for awhile, and they finally put it all into this fantastic book – which is particularly useful to pioneering business owners.

These examples are by no means meant to represent all the media to be found related to remote working, but they certainly are notable milestones of how these concepts reached the public domain.

As far back as 2002 – if you're willing to search hard enough – you can find articles and personal blog posts that hint at remote working in various ways. Sometimes they're simple telecommuters who are hacking the system, and sometimes they're entrepreneurs trying something different.

Nearly *all* of them share a sense of reticence about publicly sharing their unusual practices—we're talking about a time in which the 40-hour office *slog* was a pillar of upper-middle-class pride.

Whatever form of working away from the office, I think the one thing we can all agree upon is that they all represent a very real paradigm-shift that seems inevitable at this point in the digital tide.

After working nomadically for 10 years, I experienced this first-hand while working at a decade-old design agency in California: on the company's tenth anniversary, we unanimously decided to stop doing client work, completely decentralize, start peddling our own software, and level the playing field by making every single employee a partner. 75% of us moved far away and guess what? It worked a treat. Shocker.

Doing something like this in the age of Mad Men would have been worse than unthinkable. But if you think about it, the time is right. It's about *generations*. With most of us tech business owners in our 30's and 40's, we're old enough and have grown enough now that the crazy ideas we had years ago are now being thrust into reality.

You can't ignore Mark Zuckerberg or Jason Fried any more that you can ignore Bill Gates. Nowadays people like Jason and Zuck are more modern voices than Gates. The times have changed. *We're going to have our cake and eat it too. Because now it's us who are creating the things that demand attention.*

A common topic that arises in discussions of remote working (or its counterparts) is *lifestyle*. The digital boom opened the gates of opportunity in more ways than one; namely that – since everything else is changing – why not improve the work/life balance as well? Sure why not.

We're not the employees anymore, we're the CEOs and Founders, and we write the rules now. So we will have our cold-brew coffee and our 11am start and our pie-in-the-sky ideals. We never liked offices anyway – those were for our parents – so let's not waste money on them. Let's find people who are like-minded and go for it. They're in London and we're in Long Beach? No problem because the internet—which a lot of us build for a living.

Basecamp is a great example of this; Jason Fried and David Heinemeier Hansson simply recognized their own need for the software, and then built it for themselves. It just so happened that lots of others needed it, too.

They created their own corner of the internet that enabled them (and their employees) to work remotely. It is truly a digital age.

The term *remote working* really broke ground around 2005, and now we have big corporations considering the benefits of mass decentralization. On a practical level, the only thing holding back the entire dam from bursting is the traditional bank hours. Once we realize that we don't need to crossover our schedules for 8 hours a day, everything will change.

But back then I wasn't thinking about any of this. I considered myself a normal person running a business which couldn't afford its own office, who luckily didn't mind that fact, and was simply making do with the resources I had.

DESIGNING
EXPERIENCES

Through Ruth's connections at church, I met Richard—a founding partner at a "User Experience" (UX) agency. They were in need of a designer to help inject design into their "product".

While we sat at Café Nero discussing the role, Richard tried to explain what it was they were doing, but none of it really made sense to me until my first week there. We agreed on a 6-month contract in which I would act as the Interim Creative Director.

At the time, my work was squarely in the evolving practice of *graphic* design. At that time, most of us graphic designers came out of the print design world and were working hard at going digital. I was just ahead of that wake.

The graphic design world was still all about marketing, communication and 'solutions' – that was our modern interpretation of the traditional ad-agency mindset – the actual *reasons* behind our design decisions were usually led by creative and artistic ideas rather than science and research.

Someone once called the practice of User Experience Design *the study of the obvious*—and it is. For example, while I was telling my clients *this button is there because that's where it looks best,* Richard and his team were telling them *this button is there because, based on our user tests, that's where users will expect it to be, and therefore will qualitatively maximize the amount of appropriate clicks it receives.*

User Experience Design is the science and research behind the decisions of design and human interaction. It was an entirely fascinating world to me. It was as if *everything I had been thinking about in my own work suddenly had a context around it,* and I wasn't crazy.

I had comfortably settled into this crowd of brains at the office; I think everyone was a PHD graduate, mostly in Human-Computer Interaction (HCI). I was surrounded by people who could tell me the scientific reasoning behind the design decisions I had been making for the last 5 years of my professional life. I found myself constantly in-awe. I dug my heels in and learned as much as I could.

My 6-month contract turned into 9 months, followed by subsequent moonlighting. While working there I got to design user experiences for Ebay, lastminute.com and expedia.com to name a few. All of the user tests, research, findings and articles didn't stop at just software. I, of course, took every bit of information and applied it to nomadic working.

Now I was considering the *usability* of my bag and clothes, the *accessibility* of my cycling routes, the *progressive engagement* with my own clients. I had learned how to conduct guerrilla research on the streets, and I became more perceptive of how the little things each day were making or breaking my own 'user experience'. The applications are endless, and to this day I think of most things in my life from the perspective of 'designing' a good UX.

DISCOVERING STRATEGY

Working at Starbucks became stale, but not before I had learned a few key things.

During my time of working there, little niggling difficulties became apparent to me. I would run out of battery on my laptop and my charger was at home, or I needed my graphic tablet for some task but it was next to my charger.

Some days I would pack everything I thought I might need, but carrying it all around would make my back sore and put more pressure on my tender Californian feet (which were already being stressed to their limits).

I would recognize the need for the "loo" in the middle of working, and have to pack up my things and go (which would inevitably result in losing my seat and sometimes my coffee). I wasn't comfortable leaving my laptop unguarded for any amount of time.

If I did bring my charger, I would often have to ask people to move out of the way so I could plug it in (if a plug was nearby at all), and oftentimes Starbucks' wifi would slow down dramatically or quit altogether, forcing me to relocate.

Even at the best of times I would find myself sitting impatiently while large uploads and downloads took place, which seemed to coincide with my day coming to an end or needing the loo again.

Coffee was becoming expensive and starting to give me the jitters and my back and shoulders would start throbbing after hours in those hard wooden chairs.

More than once the following alignment of planets occurred: I packed up from my seat to stretch and get a coffee refill, only to turn around a couple minutes later – new coffee in-hand – to find that every single seat was now taken. When I'd arrive at another Starbucks I'd feel obliged to buy a new coffee, resulting in wasted money and coffee.

Those are just a few examples of the things I became aware of.

After what felt like weeks and weeks of "pushing through", the luster of Starbucks escaped me and I found myself being just as critical as when I left my own dining room weeks earlier. I needed to make a change if I was going to remain a viable and productive business owner.

I couldn't keep becoming this terribly frustrated every few months. *I'm a creative person,* I thought, *so it's time to get creative.*

E M B R A C I N G
S T R A T E G Y

On a surface-level, I began thinking about how to address these problems. The first thing I did was implement a new rule: *plug in whenever possible*. I was running out of charge on my phone and computer too often.

This was to be my first rule of many to come, but I didn't know it yet. There were so many things I tried, but this rule is a good example of what they looked like in practicality.

It wasn't as easy as it sounded—after all, there was a reason I wasn't already doing it. Most of the time it was inconvenient to plug in at all, let alone find a seat next to a plug. I hated cables cluttering my workspace. But after time of practice, I saw that this simple rule alleviated a lot of potential stress and logistical issues, and it eventually became a habit.

After practicing this for a week or so, I rarely ran out of power, and I got over my discomfort of asking people to move so I could plug in. I realized that everyone understood and happily obliged. It didn't always prevent me from running down my batteries, but it resolved the overall issue to an acceptable degree.

I also didn't try that hard; I didn't waste my time waiting for a seat next to a plug, or going to a different place for a plug. If I couldn't plug in, I just didn't. But when I could, I did so religiously. My first rule was working, so I kept going with my experiments.

This isn't that hard, I thought, and it introduced a sort of 'bigger picture' into my typical work-day.

Ruth and I would meet for lunch in town, go shopping together or just meet over a coffee wherever I was. Since we both didn't work from an office and had plenty of freedom, it was nice to be able to see each other regularly throughout the day.

Working in-town, I took several opportunities to go for little walks and learn the streets. I became familiar with Bristol's City Center, and I really loved the quirky European things about it; cobblestone streets, terraced buildings, quaint little shops and the myriad of 'mis-spellings' like *practise, theatre* and English greetings like "Hiya" and "alright?".

(...which does not mean *"Are you all right?"*—The first time Ruth said this to me I thought to myself *Oh no! Has something terrible happened that I should be aware of?*) I still don't really know what *alright?* means, even though I adopted it myself eventually. I think the closest approximation in Californian might be *how's it going?*

STRATEGY
TO RESEARCH

With all the walking, my feet were hurting every day. The Wallaby knock-offs I had purchased months earlier already had holes in the bottom which let rainwater keep my feet cold and wet.

I started researching shoes that would let me get more miles in a day with less discomfort and more warmth, might last longer and offer some level of protection from rain (which of course was a common occurrence).

My motivation to do any research came from three circumstances: Firstly, that my feet and back were in pain every day. Secondly, I realized that even though I "got a deal", the pair of shoes I was wearing were not a good choice. I knew I needed a longer-term view of what my days were going to be.

To my Californian mind, I literally thought *Ok, so I have to pretend I'm going to be hiking all day in the rain for a year with little or no help.* And thirdly, I couldn't afford to waste money again on something that wouldn't work. My research left me settled on a pair of Merrell Chameleon II's and I went shopping.

Though I was a little better off financially, I still had a hard time justifying the price. They were £65 GBP, which in those days meant more than $100 USD. Not cheap—especially for a particularly ugly shoe. But the level and frequency of discomfort I had been experiencing helped me justify the cost. I purchased a brand new pair at a local shoe store on Park Street and wore them out the door. Time eventually proved that this was to be my second #win.

This example – while 100% true – is also purposefully trite. The tiny, seemingly innocuous things can make the biggest impact. Simply thinking through which pair of shoes I aught to buy improved a big part of my daily experience.

Had I been *driving* everywhere instead of walking in those days, then I might have focused instead on changing tires or saving on gas—I don't know. Every single time I addressed something it was always on a case-by-case basis; *identify, research, experiment, apply.* That's what I did over and over with issues large and small. Rarely did it require specialized knowledge or any special skill other than *using the internet like a boss.*

The real key here is the first step; *identify.* I've noticed that most people never get to this part. They'll have some issue, get frustrated, and then forget about it until it happens again. Rinse and repeat this recipe for fully-baked frustration.

I'd like my rocket surgery diploma now, please.

RESEARCH TO EXPERIMENTS

With Ruth and I wanting to improve the house, we decided to try and save up some money. I started watching every pound spent on coffee and food at cafés. I didn't want to stop working away from home, so I needed to find a way to make it more affordable.

The first thing I did was to start being more mindful of my purchases. I stopped buying any expensive lattes or sandwiches and started buying "filter" coffee (not espresso). I put £10 on a Starbucks Card after learning that it saved me 10p on each purchase and allowed me to have free refills.

Some of these little problems were no-brainers, and simple logic like this was enough to make a significant improvement. Like I said – nomadic working is just being consciously strategic about things you already know – hardly anything is truly 'new'.

I did the same at Boston Tea Party, Café Gusto, Café Nero and Lashings Café. Each had their own rewards system, and the frequency of my visits began to re-align themselves according to how much money their rewards programs were saving me. With a tiny bit of effort in managing physical cards I started saving about £10 each day compared to the previous week. As a side-benefit, this juggle led me to change up my rota a bit.

For lunch, I started shopping around a little instead of buying whatever my current café was offering. Around noon each day, I would wrap up work and leave my current location to look for a new lunch deal nearby.

I tried everything from Subway to McDonald's to £3 Sushi lunches to the street "kebab" carts. I was leaving the café because they rarely had any good lunch deals, and I knew I could find better food deals elsewhere. Food at cafés was always overpriced. Leaving the café became a habit that was easy to build. #easywin

While I was now spending far less on lunch, I noticed I was getting tired quicker than usual after eating, and this was affecting productivity.

Many of the options I was trying were unhealthy fast-foods, and the price of their convenience was costing me more than just productivity—my general health was suffering.

Saving a few pounds (as in Pounds Sterling) wasn't worth compromising my overall experience. Nomadic working – like anything else – is easier when you feel good physically. I added *Health and energy* to my mental list.

So I kept on leaving my café at noon in search of new lunch options, but now I was being conscious of which foods I was eating.

The simple choice of a sushi plate instead of a slice of pizza, or a veggie-packed sub instead of a plate of curry-covered "chips" made all the difference, and still let me save money each day. I had my energy and my money, for the second #win that week.

These are just a few more trite examples meant to diffuse any misunderstanding about what nomadic working actually looks like. There is no manual, formula or best-practice. There's no magical quality one must possess in order to become a nomadic worker (though a severe case of *Ricky-Bobby Syndrome* helps).

And like this time, solving one issue sometimes inadvertently spawns a new one, and other times has unforeseen positive effects.

The difference between *me* running down the battery of my laptop at Starbucks and someone else doing it is that I chose to be conscious of it and strategically address it so it wouldn't happen again. Yes, it's that simple.

I know—it's stupid. These are the stupid little problems that many of us experience on a daily basis, not some giant 5-year plan that must be followed to a T before seeing any success. It's easy. Anyone can do it. Results are often immediate, and progress comes easily. If it was hard I probably wouldn't be writing this.

It doesn't take long before they all start adding up, and that's when things get even more enjoyable. Suddenly, work sessions are uninterrupted by these kinds of minor (but frequent) annoyances; it's a cumulative effect.

Productivity goes up because interruptions become less frequent, inspiration is easily found and physical and mental health contribute all-round.

I completed *Health and energy* on my list, and then started on the new item that this recent experiment had spawned—*taking breaks.*

BURNOUTS
AND BREAKS

All business owners will tell you that you're never really "off".
As the person solely responsible for pretty much everything,
there's always a new problem to fix or a new bit of work
to complete. Without anyone hovering over your shoulder or a
time card to punch, it's easier than anything to do a 60-hour week
without blinking.

But we all know you can't do this forever, and *burning out* is a very
real thing that I was learning first-hand. I burned out many times,
even after learning to take breaks.

For me it was often down to the 'creative process'—I would get
inspired for something and work tirelessly for 8-12 hours each
day until the creative streak was exhausted. Usually this took a few
days, but sometimes it was a few weeks.

Ruth could always tell when I burned out because I would get
irritable or stay in bed for 14 hours. I'd binge-watch TV or force
myself to take a day off by visiting London without a computer.

Even though taking advantage of creative streaks caused me to
burn out, I don't regret doing it. When a streak comes along, you've
got to exploit it for all it's worth. Routines and regularity won't ever
have a problem returning, but *inspiration* is a precious gem that

deserves attention.

During my *health and energy* experiments I noticed these more dedicated lunches having the residual effect of leaving me refreshed and focused by the time I got back to work. If my meal was light and healthy, it became much easier to get through the rest of the day feeling productive.

Contrarily, if I slipped back into an old habit of grabbing a sandwich without leaving the café where I'd been working and instead continued to work straight through lunch, my energy and productivity would peak early, around 4pm.

The fact that I was eating healthier made me feel better physically and mentally, but the distinctive break in-itself was heavily contributing to my day's success. This was an unplanned, unforeseen benefit.

On top of that, I was able to spend more dedicated time with Ruth over lunches, during which my mind wasn't still hard at work. I looked at how the characteristics of my previous habits compared to my new, dedicated lunch breaks:

These new breaks featured a different atmosphere that never included work. This made it easier to pull my brain away from work projects, and instead write a poem, read a book, or simply enjoy my food slowly. 30 or 60 minutes of productivity time removed from my routine (in the form of a break) resulted in the entire second-half of my day being inspired, focused and feeling great, giving me a net-gain of almost 2 full hours of better productivity by 6pm.

The huge gain from such a simple change was astonishing to me, and I wondered if I could take it further.

After a little research into the topic I added several items to my list: *Sleep, physical breaks, mental breaks, naps,* and *foods for energy.* My experiments with each of these were wide and varied, and I won't go into detail. But as you might imagine, after a month or so of experimentation and more learning, I got to the point where I was starting work at 7am, cruising through with a couple conscious breaks until lunch, then a 90-minute dedicated down-time while eating, and then repeating the morning routine until 6pm.

On a daily basis I was walking between places about 5 times and covering between 5 and 15 miles. I never worked for more than 2 hours at a time without taking at least a 30 minute break.

I took lots of breaks because it was almost as if for every 30 minutes of relaxation I gained an hour of solid productivity. Unsurprisingly, the traditional western 40-hour work week is not necessarily the way to be the most productive.

With this new regime I had cut my actual production hours to about 5 per day while taking more breaks and getting far more work completed to a higher degree of quality. I had traded in 8 hours of "pushing through" for 5 hours of inspired productivity and 3 hours of relaxation.

The end-result was a week that was far more relaxing and nearly twice as productive, which meant I was working faster and therefore billing and getting paid faster, too.

This improvement also had a positive effect on life with Ruth. My workdays were more productive and energetic, which let me meet with Ruth that evening feeling positive and like work was complete. I was finishing early a lot. I was able to fully set work aside in my mind and invest into our relationship together more often than not.

In fact, this crazy thing I was doing had a way of constantly spilling over into the rest of my life. I realized it's not just about work, but that these experiments were having a direct effect on everything else I cared about.

This realization changed the way I looked at my habit of *strategic experimentation,* and now I approached everything in the context of my entire lifestyle. It's not like Ruth and I constantly discussed nomadic working, but it's residual effects on my life were more than tangible, and often a welcome change.

This is why when I talk about nomadic working today, a word that often comes up is *wholeness.* Nomadic working, for me, became a way to be productive and happy at work while actually improving the rest of my life. It's a lifestyle that embraces today's increasingly blurred boundaries between life and work in order to help both be not just sustainable, but full of inspiration and adventure.

It's a "whole" view of life, and that's why I don't call it a *working* method or some other new trend to boost company morale, but an entirely *whole* way in which to 'design' one's lifestyle.

Nomadic working does not allow a strong distinction between life and work, but rather, it blurs the boundary between them by making both more rich and rewarding.

That's not to say that nomadic working is a singular and comprehensive answer to any problem one might encounter, but rather it's a way to bring work and life together in a more harmonious way. Nomadic working focuses on removing obstacles and optimizing what's already working. The end result should be inspiration, adventure and productivity.

While we're on the subject, I want to address a very valid question that often arises at this point in the discussion: *is blurring the boundary between work and life a 'good' thing?* I'm glad you asked.

Not everyone thinks so. For me, the answer is yes. And I suspect that my answer lies in the fact that I love what I do for work. Not everyone does, unfortunately. But I do. My work is something I care about and enjoy, and because of that, I want it to be a part of the rest of my life (and vice-versa).

I don't know if nomadic working is suitable for those who don't enjoy their work because I've never experienced that combination for myself. But I'd love to know the answer.

If I can project a little, I also suspect that nomadic working might be a way in which one could *make* their work more enjoyable, because in my experience, nomadic working improves every area of life.

DESIGN INSTRUCTION

I found myself getting into an unusual rhythm. I was getting up early to take advantage of the quiet morning hours in town and I would finish all my work by 2 or 3pm. Most days I would switch to a side-project and work on it for a few hours before heading home. Some days I'd go home early and Ruth and I would do something if she could take the time off.

But in this routine I got to a point where my side-projects were 'done', and those last 3 hours of the day started to be hard to fill.

It was a 'slow day' and I had walked that morning. On my way home I passed the same higher-education campus I had passed a million times before. But this time, I went in. I don't know why, I think I just wanted to see what they were up to. This little campus in the ghetto was about a block from our house, right on my route into town.

I went in and was greeted by a third-generation Jamaican called Kevin. He was very eloquent and clean-cut, with a modern flair of creativity about him.

I told Kevin I was just walking by, that I was a designer and just wanted to see what was happening here. His eyes lit up, and he explained that the school was run completely by volunteers because the government had cut their funding a couple years prior. They were "just trying to make it work", and I perceived that it wasn't going as well as Kevin had hoped.

In that building, volunteers were teaching music, singing, fine art, video production, graphic design and web design. The building was on the government list for 'subsidized' and that's the only break they got. They were paying their own utilities and finding volunteers to teach classes. It seemed as though it was a match made in heaven.

I had taught design before at businesses, but never for an actual school. I told Kevin that I had some extra time on my hands for the foreseeable future and that I'd be happy to take on a couple courses.

We sat down to discuss curriculum, teaching style and my background in design. Before I left I was the new instructor of *Introduction to Web Design* and *Intermediate Graphic Design* at this little accredited campus.

The school had been setup to take all the government-funded 'students' that other, more popular schools didn't want. Classes were two-and-a-half hours in the morning, and the students ranged from 25-year-old miscreants fulfilling a court sentence to 60-year-old pensioners on the dole looking for a way to get out of the system and back into the working world. I simply shifted my daily schedule 3 hours back to teach these classes.

I don't know the ins and outs of how Kevin managed everything; how bills were being paid etc. I know he was in talks with the education funding council constantly, but he never shared that with me, and I never asked.

A few times he offered to put me on a salary, but each time I declined because I knew that as soon as I was being paid, it would no longer be me 'giving', and that was important to me. I was doing it because it helped others and I enjoyed it. And I didn't really need the amount of money that would have probably been offered.

I taught those two classes for two consecutive school years. I got to know the students well, and learned each of their stories. I learned that most of them were our neighbors to some degree, and I enjoyed the opportunity to better understand some of their individual situations. It brought me closer to my neighborhood with a fresh understanding, and from then on I never felt the same way when I walked past a homeless person, a drug addict or someone on the dole.

Just like my time on the streets in Huntington Beach, this experience helped re-align my nature to be more grounded and less presumptuous.

Spending this small amount of time directly investing into others was such an enriching experience for me. I always looked forward to class and making sure everyone was really learning. I enjoyed it so much that even today I'd openly consider teaching design once again.

It also dawned on me that nomadic working had led me into a position in which I had something to give, and I felt as though my new role as an instructor was teaching *me* more than anyone else.

It became easier to love people. I went about my days with a feeling of peaceful humility that I was able to invest into my own community, and directly affect the lives of my own neighbors. I was experiencing the truth that giving brings more joy than receiving, and it felt great.

ENGLAND VS CALIFORNIA

I mentioned *frequent rain* in England, and that it was an entirely new problem to me. Back in California, rain was never an issue because the entire state is designed to drive from door-to-door with ample free parking everywhere. It's easy to avoid the rain, and in Orange County we get more than the rest of SoCal.

Everyone has a car, and you can't really survive the state without one. I no longer had a car, and I hated the bus because the prices were extortionate for the serially unreliable service they provided in Bristol.

Most days I was walking through the rain and simply getting wet. The cheap umbrella I had purchased a few weeks earlier had broken (I hated carrying it anyway.) If I was lucky enough to walk beneath awnings and tunnels so as to not soak through to my base layer, that was considered a victory by the time I stripped off my outer layer at my café of choice. If I was lucky, that outer layer would have dried by the time I ventured back out into the rain.

This time, I skipped the research and just went shopping. I knew exactly what I needed: a simple, waterproof "shell" jacket with a hood. I entered Debenham's and exited with an £85 water-resistant shell from The North Face and was very happy with myself.

I wore that jacket every day for months, but *it was not the right choice.*

The jacket didn't breathe at all, so now instead of entering a café soaked with *rain,* I was entering it soaked from the inside-out with *sweat* whether it was raining or not. I had spent £85 and actually made my problem worse, and with money being a tight, it hurt. In the hardest way, I learned that *research is always necessary.*

That's one example of the trials and errors I experienced in that first year in England. With so many new variables in weather, temperature, culture and my business, the list seemed endless. A little #win would keep me going, and then ten more difficulties would make my list. I wanted to make faster progress so I didn't have to go back to working from my dining room.

So for a moment I want to talk about the mindset I had which helped me push through some of these rare-but-frustrating moments of nomadic working.

The fact that I didn't like being at home made it a little easier for me to stick it out. Even when I was frustrated, I looked forward to getting into town each morning before work.

If all else failed, I had so many fall-back options by that point that it never really mattered; I could always go to any number of my favorite places and predictably get a work session. The knowledge I had accumulated made the whole thing very low-risk. That is the nature of what nomadic working builds—the longer you do it, the lower your risk becomes.

What risk? you might ask... the risk of having a bad experience or productivity being interrupted. Whether it's a laptop dying, rain, uncomfortable shoes or shoddy wifi – these are the little things that accumulate into an under-productive and bad working experience.

The more you identify, research, experiment and apply those findings, the lower your risk becomes. *Don't ignore the little things.*

In looking back, I realize the fact that I never stopped going out every day was key. I was constantly eager to discover new rules, methods, routes and products that would either make my life somehow easier, or enable me to enjoy it more.

As you've seen, little things like learning to take regular, intentional breaks, or eating well, or trying out a new place to work for a fresh sense of adventure were the things that made me love it.

If I had given up and stayed home – especially after a frustrating problem arose – it might have been easy to start building another home office (probably only to repeat the cycle again).

Deep down, though, I knew that no matter how convenient or fancy any home office might have been, it would never be able to supply this great sense of discovery of a new location, or the inspiration of the wilderness, or the satisfaction that accompanied a unique solution. Nomadic working had so much more to offer, and I had already tasted too much of it to give up now.

Meanwhile, I noticed another thing happening to me. I was no longer wearing skin-tight jeans, doing my hair in the morning or caring about those things in the least bit. What happened!?

The "Designer" image I had carefully crafted back in California had crumbled away, and I didn't care in the least. I was being hardened by a harsher environment.

Since I had moved to Bristol, I suddenly couldn't control getting dirty in the rain, or having to 'push through' one thing or another on a daily basis. The refined and controlled personality from Pomona had given way to something entirely new.

My clothes were now being chosen for their utility before their fashion. I was getting dirty every day and it wasn't bothering me. That physical side of just getting 'stuck in' to life had become a reality before I could considered whether or not I wanted it to happen.

This is great! I thought. Having grown up in such a controlled, effeminate environment, this was nothing short of a revelation to me. My physical appearance was changing from my previous *Tinkerbell silhouette* to a more roughly-hewn *"yep—that's definitely a male of the species. Perhaps a young lumberjack."* I felt like I had earned my Man Card or something, and suddenly the skinny designer from California seemed like a sad historical joke that made me smile.

When it really came down to it, I loved how my experience of nomadic working in England was shaping me, both inside and out.

BROADER HORIZONS

Back into the swing of things and with Starbucks barely a memory, I continued branching out to other cafés, media centers, and I even tried working at a pub and various covered outdoor areas.

During my love affair with Starbucks I had inadvertently cobbled together a mental list of which ones had fast or reliable wifi, which ones kept the creamer topped up and things like that. New places made this mental list, which had become rather large and difficult to keep track of.

With my new shoes I was covering more distance and add new places to my repertoire. In Bristol, it seemed like the artsy culture had new and interesting establishments opening every week.

The shabby-chic Boston Tea Party café became a personal favorite, as did Goldbrick House (for when I felt like treating myself a little). I became fearless when trying new places. I learned to expect anomalies and to a degree, flow around them. That summer, I probably visited close to a hundred different options within central Bristol. The monotony of working every day in the same place had gone, and I counted this as a huge overall #win.

In the spring and summer I spent time working at outdoor cafés a lot. I had made a few friends with whom I could meet for lunch, and would often have chance encounters with them throughout the city. I loved being in control of my own schedule.

At times these encounters were welcome breaks from work, and other times it was hard to pull myself away and I counted them as interruptions. On busy days I got into the habit of working from lesser-known places a little farther from civilization where I would lower my chances of interruption, but most days I welcomed and enjoyed these impromptu meetings with people I loved.

Work was becoming more collaborative as I worked with other professionals and agencies. I made some great friends doing that, and began to re-carve my own niche with work. I became known as many different things; *the Wordpress guy, the designer who codes* and so on. I was building a reputation in Bristol's rich creative scene, and it kept leading to more work as word traveled.

I would be asked to join an agency in their office for a week or two for specific projects or I would take a long-term contract here and there. But most of the time I spent my days across Bristol bumping into friends and working on private-client projects as well as my own personal projects.

The rhythm of life was very agreeable, with a constantly shifting balance of work, life, friends and family. The freedom to explore every day and gain fresh inspiration left me wanting little.

If I settled a little too deeply into a routine, a contract would start and break up the monotony. If I spent too much time with friends the previous week, I would take all that extra emotional energy and invest into work the next.

TIME HEALS
ALL WOUNDS

I was in the groove. Nomadic working had become second-nature.
I loved how it helped to balance my life. I was inspired enough
to do good design work. I had energy to invest into my life with
Ruth when I got home. I felt pretty good physically, and nomadic
working had inadvertently carved out enough extra time for me to
invest into side projects.

I was sitting at The Watershed Media Centre one day as I answered
a call from an "unknown" caller. It was Dad. I hadn't really spoken
with him for years, and we hadn't had a meaningful conversation
since I'd run away from home that sad day in Orange County.

"Hi son it's dad" he said. (He always calls me 'son', which I find kind
of endearing.) *"I was just thinking about you. I've got a few minutes
before my next pickup and Kelli helped me figure out how to dial your
number from out here."*

At the time, Dad and Kelli were driving a big-rig truck all across
The States, delivering stuff all over the place. They were seeing the
far corners of the US for the first time. They'd bought a couple
Honda Goldwing motorcycles to ride cross-country on the
weekends & holidays. Years had gone by and they had really settled
into a good life, and they were happy.

"Hi dad, it's good to hear from you." I managed to get out. For some reason I felt that same feeling I had felt 15 years earlier when I decided to move in with him; *I just need my dad.* I welled up inside and it hit me that we had so much time behind us—it had been years since I had run away from home.

We were both in completely different stages of life now, and it all felt like water under the bridge, even though I had come to deeply regret the pain I had caused with that single decision. Dad's knack for showing tireless love had remained, and I remembered all the ways in which I admired him, and wanted to be like him.

Over the next 15 minutes we talked about what we both were doing. We talked about Ruth and Kelli. We talked about our jobs, and Dad asked about where we had traveled. I told him I had just been back from a trip up to Dundee, Scotland and he said how much he had wanted to see Scotland. He asked me about my time in Austria, Paris, Barcelona and of course England.

He did a couple Monty-Python-esque impressions of Ruth and we both laughed. He was always good at accents, and his time on-stage performing King Lear when I was young had paid off.

I felt as though a dam had split. All my emotions flooded over me in a massive rushing wave as I said goodbye. I'll never forget how strongly I recalled my love for my dad on that simple phone call. It broke the ice for me, and from that point on my dad and I talked regularly, which we still do to this day.

He still does his English accent sometimes, and now that I think about it, I think his is the best version I've heard from an American (even if it is a little on the Cockney side).

Being back in touch with my father somehow helped me process all the change that I was going through as a person, and I realized that some of Dad's traits I had revered over the years had stayed with me and even come to the surface, and that thought made me very happy.

WORKING OUTDOORS

Having spent my time hopping from one place to the next, it occurred to me that working away from home offered a sense of being "out in the wild" that was enough for awhile, but I wanted more inspiration.

Back in California I found it in two primary places; looking at the creative works of others, and spending time outdoors. With my professional focus having shifted me away from the creative works of others, *the outdoors* remained the only natural alternative.

But this was England, not sunny California. I knew working outdoors wasn't going to be easy. Rain seemed to come without a moment's notice. I would need to learn the patterns so I could predict them more effectively and be better prepared when my predictions failed.

I started simply, with what I knew; outdoor café tables and local parks. I even setup a table in my own backyard a couple times when the rain let up. Just between cafés and parks there was a huge range of options at my disposal, and it changed the way I judged a café.

Now I was looking at their outdoor offerings—not just how comfy their chairs looked or how many chairs they had. Summer was coming to an end, so it was a good time to start exploring before the rain returned to its typical regularity.

Most of the time it was simply a case of sitting *outside* the café instead of inside. Parks were a little more involved; most of the time there was no protection from the elements, plus it was usually a little chilly. For good reason, seeing people working outside in England wasn't a common occurrence except for the odd occasion during unusually warm days.

Outdoor café tables proved to be a relatively simple challenge for the most part; except that they were very small and often situated on a busy sidewalk with people passing within inches of me like Manhattan during Christmas season. Foot-traffic was always heavy, and I found the lack of personal space so distracting that I eventually sought out the lesser-trafficked outdoor cafés across Bristol.

With many of the outdoor café tables, their small surface area seemed to be a common feature, and it only took one or two instances before I moused off the edge of the table every few minutes. It was like falling asleep on a train and being awoken by a bump – just as you nod off – over and over again. My hand started hurting from gripping the mouse more tightly to avoid further instances of dropping it to the ground, exploding into a hodgepodge of batteries and battery doors, and then having to excuse myself for the disturbance as I collected my parts from under people's feet.

Stationary mouse made it to my list that day, and the first break I got, I began searching online and reading various reviews. A few days later I made a decision to buy a "trackball" mouse made by Logitech and I purchased the best deal I could find online.

(A *trackball* mouse is a computer mouse which has a large ball that you move with a finger. The mouse itself never moves during use, which solved my surface-area problem.)

Using the trackball-style mouse took a day of patience, but I quickly acclimated to it, being surprised at how much more comfortable it was all day compared to my old mouse.

I marked the list-item complete on my mental list. To this day I have replaced this mouse with the same model twice more. I'm on my ~~third~~ *fourth* one now, the Logitech M570 (but this first one was it's wired predecessor).

It's always the simple, practical changes that make the biggest impact in nomadic working. The mouse is a good example because it's something I used every day, literally for hours on-end. Many other items fell into this category like shoes, bags, routes and transportation, so strategically thinking about each of them was a pretty obvious path for improvement, like the internet problem...

The constant problem with working at cafés was their internet connections. They were predictably slow and unreliable, which was particularly an issue if it was a new-to-me café whose wifi temperament I hadn't yet become familiar with and could therefore not predict or plan around. This problem was common at cafés, but parks would be an entirely different challenge.

Thankfully the solutions to these problems coincided quite nicely...

A STEP FROM CIVILIZATION

At a park, fighting the wifi connection wasn't even an option, because there was none. With more than half of my work being web-based projects, I couldn't afford to be without an internet connection for more than an hour or so, and those hours were rare.

I had found a small community park in the same neighborhood as our house at Number 7. It was beautiful and quiet with benches, a comically small skatepark and a couple kids' jungle-gyms. I setup shop at a bench and – with seemingly no other option – tethered my phone for an internet connection.

After doing this with reasonable success for a couple days I received an automated email from Vodafone informing me that I exceeded my data allowance for the entire month! I hadn't been in the habit of tethering very often for a connection, and I knew now that it wouldn't be an option at all. I didn't like the idea of spending more money every month to increase my phone's data plan or buy some dedicated internet USB "dongle".

I started to feel a little down. I didn't want to give up my newfound experience of working outdoors and I had fallen in love with this location, but practical realities were challenging it, and without any apparent solutions. This was the first problem I came up against which lacked a light at the end of the tunnel.

I started a bit of Googling which, at first, revealed no more than I already knew: paid wifi network subscriptions, dongles and other devices with a monthly plan, a larger phone data plan and the like. Such were the offerings back in those pre-iPhone days when tethering a phone required a degree in computer science.

Then I happened upon a blog comment mentioning *USB wifi antenna*. These three words piqued my interest; If there was a way I could simply *extend* the range of my computer's wifi, then surely I would find an open network—I was in the middle of the city after all, and surrounded by homes and businesses. My laptop did have wifi built-in, but it wasn't strong enough to see more than a couple password-protected networks surrounding the park.

I refocused my Google search and discovered a smallish company in The States called *Quickertek*. They make a device that is basically a big-ass wifi antenna on the end of a USB cable, with a little metal box in-between. It drew power from USB in order to extend the wifi range several times over. I wasn't willing to pay an additional £80/mo. for some dongle or data plan, but I could easily justify $100 USD once-off on a more permanent solution.

Normally I would have started a spreadsheet comparing all the aspects of each competitor on the market before making a decision about spending so much money. Problem was, I couldn't find a single other company making anything even remotely similar.

With the single option, I pulled the trigger. It would be on my doorstep from America in a week.

As with most other online orders I made, I eagerly awaited

its arrival. The following Monday a FedEx Global box graced the hidden spot behind our 'bin' next to the front door.

Grateful that it hadn't been stolen, I tore it open, installed the software and immediately walked back to that park for my first trial. I sat at my bench, opened my laptop and plugged in my Quicky USB wifi antenna.

Clicking *Scan for Networks* revealed far more than the typical 2 networks I had seen during previous visits. The list was so long that it needed to scroll it to see everything. Page after page of available networks. Most were protected, but the network at the pub down the road was left open for customers. From that day on, I enjoyed a fast and reliable wifi connection every time I visited that park.

It's worth mentioning that I was very conscious about "stealing" internet. It didn't sit well with me, and I made sure to closely watch my usage. The last thing I wanted was to have some elderly couple who use their internet for emailing their grandkids to get a big bill they weren't expecting.

In fact, even curtailing my usage felt like a cop-out. Sure—they should have secured their networks, but really, it would be far better to use a local business' connection because they've at least planned for a huge number of people to use their public networks. I was a regular customer at most of them, anyway.

Being tucked away and unpopular, the pub's network was always snappy. I was probably the only one using it. Because it was so nearby, that pub became another nice quiet place to escape the weather over a lukewarm pint of Boddingtons.

The *Quicky* is, I think, one of the best examples of really thinking outside the box when nomadic working. There was a reason this company seemed small, because there wasn't a huge need. I had never before heard of such a product existing, and yet this small investment was going to cut the internet cord that had been chaining me to cafés this whole time.

From that point on, I was no longer tethered to brick-and-mortar shops because about 85% of the time, I could get a wifi signal from anywhere I went inside the city. I avoided any monthly bills and stopped worrying about being able to find connections wherever I stopped. The Quicky was a hammer that broke yet another chain of being tied down in some way to common working practices.

Huge #win noted. I was untethered from shops and even public places in-general. I used the Quicky for 7 years while it lasted through 3 new laptops. People regularly asked me about it, and my enthusiasm probably sold several more of them over the years.

During the move to Colorado I broke the antenna, and happily went online to order the latest model, which has served me even better. I can't recommend it enough as a core connectivity tool for nomadic working... it's one of the few products I often rave about.

If I hadn't engaged in that open-minded, 'blind' research, I may have never been free to venture away from civilization. Funny how the littlest things can have such a practical impact.

STRATEGY APPEARS

With my boredom of cafés cured, I freed up the mental space to tackle some of the remaining larger issues I faced every day; my gear getting wet from rain seeping through my backpack, arriving at each place soaked with sweat, and walking from place-to-place taking up more of my work hours and physical energy than I wanted to spend.

My mental list found its way to a text document on my Nokia e90 phone. Once I really settled into the habit of updating this list, it grew at a rate that I never would have expected. Seeing it all right in front of me 'on-paper' made it feel so real. There really were *so many things* that needed to be addressed.

Here's a portion of one of my early lists, before they needed to be reigned-in:

- `Starbucks on Park Street rammed w/ students from 3-7pm`

- `WATERPROOF BAG!`

- `Physically exhausted by 3pm, feet hurt`

by 4pm. WALK LESS! route plan?

- Laptop full, make space or external HD

- anyone make wireless graphic tablet?

- get podcasts on phone for walking

- PLUG IN PHONE!

- Starbucks Card, BTP card

- research gloves, jacket & thermals

At first, these notes were just plain text bullets confined to my phone. The first iPhone had just been announced and was well outside my budget. Thankfully, weeks before my beloved Nokia was stolen, I had migrated them into my new Google Docs account so that I could edit them from any device, and they became more complex with nested bullets, some semblance of prioritization and links for research.

After a year of managing them on the new Google Docs, that list became unruly, and I switched to a more simple and organized to-do list in a small 'steno' notebook. I liked the tactile, analog format because it let my thoughts flow a bit more freely, and created a separate physical space from my increasingly *digital* life.

I had become consciously strategic in the way I recorded and addressed these issues. Many of them were small and simple, but inevitably speckled with much larger issues like *transportation*.

These lists would eventually prove to be an invaluable aspect of my journey's progress. After awhile with my physical notes I settled into a strategy of titling one-page-per-issue to leave room for research below, and recording each title and page number on my "#wins" page at the back once I had marked it off. This let me archive my research and easily find it later.

Eventually I began dating each page as well, which helped me look back at a timeline of progress.

Once I settled into a rhythm with my pen-and-paper system, I tried a few different stationery options; Moleskine notebooks, Field Notes notebooks, Rhodia brand notebooks, simple and cheap ones from the local office supply store.

My favorite one which I still prefer to this day is the Field Notes. The simple, high-quality design and construction suited my needs. When they're available, I prefer the waterproof "Expedition" Field Notes (after a few coffee spills and rain rendered some notes illegible). The size was perfect for any pocket, and I usually keep it in the back pocket of my jeans.

Years into this notebook method refined my simple system which I still use today. If it ain't broke…

Though everyone is different, I recommend using a *physical* notebook instead of your mobile phone or other digital device for note-taking on nomadic working. The simple physical difference makes it easy to focus on content and avoid distractions, like email and text notifications.

I won't go into any further detail of what my notebooks are like because it will (and should) be a relatively un-prescribed free-flow that differs from person to person. The main thing is that you're able to easily find the topics you need, and I would encourage you to keep a log of your #wins as they happen so you can look back and get that warm fuzzy feeling of accomplishment.

I have a stash of completed notebooks in a drawer at home now. When I start a new one, I go back through my last one and transfer the one or two unresolved issues to the front of my new book.

I lost a notebook once, but it turned out that it didn't really matter because I had become so familiar with each page that I easily performed the transfer of unresolved issues to a new book from memory—and even if I forgot one, the issue hadn't gone away and would've naturally made it's way back in.

WINTER WEDDING

In the winter of 2006 Ruth and I were married at our church on a cold and clear November afternoon. With much help from the community and on a very tight budget, we had cobbled together an event which appeared to cost ten times as much. Ruth was exceptionally skilled at doing this, having done it several times previously for various large church events.

Much of my family and friends flew out for several days and we put them up at houses and rooms volunteered by members of the church. One such house was an exquisite mansion in Abbot's Leigh—a "country" community about 7 miles outside Bristol City Centre and across Clifton Suspension Bridge.

The mansion's property featured tennis courts, a pool, a gated private drive, it's own 'wood' complete with deer and of course many luxurious bedrooms, bathrooms and living rooms spread generously over 3 levels of meticulously maintained opulence.

It's proprietors Steve & Nicky had recently become close friends of ours, having led our pre-marriage counseling sessions in the nicest room of their magnificent home. Little did we know at the time that their involvement in our lives would become so significant and precious.

For our honeymoon directly following the wedding, Ruth and I skipped off to Saléres, Spain; a tiny village nestled in the

Sierra Nevadas where we spent three weeks in a rented house. Each morning we woke up late, cooked ourselves a nice breakfast and spent time in the nearest city of Granada where we shopped and enjoyed tapas.

In all my memory of holidays and vacations, I had never before been so relaxed and happy. Spain is a beautiful country, perfect for a honeymoon, and being in the mountains was the best place for me to relax and reflect.

In our rented Citröen hatchback I rowed the gears with my left hand through the mountains as we explored the countryside. Once, we got lost in the mountains and I pulled over to ask directions from two elderly gentleman sitting on a park bench overlooking a deep, dry mountain valley. There was nothing for miles, and I still have no idea what they were doing there.

Their reply to my request for directions was *uncontrollable laughter* followed by them looking at each other and laughing again. When I asked what was so funny, the 'younger' of the two replied that *the way I spoke Spanish sounded like I had had a rough life and had just been released from prison*. For the rest of my life I would be very self-conscious about my "Mexican" Spanish.

We returned home to Bristol and Ruth permanently joined me at Number 7. My end-game was complete and a success. We spent the following weeks homemaking and began enjoying the life we had been planning together during the previous year. Feeling refreshed, I returned to my lists and adventures of 'designing' my experience of work and life.

TRANSPORT

The most incurable work issue in late 2006 was that
of *transportation*. I had built up a strong resilience to much
walking and was in decent shape despite the heavy English meals
in-between more beer than I had ever experienced.

The fact that my body was growing out of boyhood and starting
to feel tired was outpaced by my eagerness to dig deeper into my
current adventure. I was eager to know what would come next.

I had spent the better part of a year walking from place-to-place. I
knew that I was spending too much time & energy walking, but I
liked that I had plenty of exercise built into my day.

We had recently been given a car, but if you could see the traffic,
roads and parking situation in Bristol you'd realize why we rarely
used it. In fact, it only saw action for large grocery trips and visiting
Ruth's father in West Wales—trips we had done before by foot or
train, respectively.

A close friend of mine, Matt, had recently got into
fixed-gear cycling. That is, a bicycle usually without a brake or the
ability to coast, and if you pedal backward *you go backward*.

I quickly learned that this was an up-and-coming trend in
England, with plenty of hipsters involved, but I wasn't convinced
about bicycles in-general. I hadn't cycled since my youth and the

prospect of being anywhere near Bristol traffic on something so unsafe as a bicycle left me feeling uneasy. This mode of transportation seemed to address many of my needs, but I wasn't ready to commit.

We had been invited by Steve & Nicky of the Abbot's Leigh Mansion to move in with them for an undetermined amount of time, in order to give us a leg up. We unanimously jumped at the idea of having not just a *finished* place to live in, but a very nice one too.

Our car had died and been disposed of, and shortly after moving in we became intimately familiar with the bus schedule to travel the 6.5 miles into central Bristol most days. We rented our house to friends and found ourselves in a financial state with a little more breathing room.

Ruth and I had most of the first floor to ourselves. As it began to snow that winter, I made myself a makeshift desk upstairs in the Snooker Room (which doubled as the library and entrance to Nicky's sewing room). Needless to say, I learned how to play snooker and borrowed several books from Nicky's fantastic vintage sci-fi collection. Steve had an original Apple II computer that I always wanted to try out.

That Christmas, Ruth and I bought a tiny Christmas tree to decorate on our nightstand opposite the bed, and we decided to start 'trying for a baby' (that's how you're supposed to say it, right?).

We spent evenings watching films with Steve & Nicky, helped arrange the backyard wedding for their son, and spent most

Sundays having 'Sunday Lunch' with them and their guests. Steve & Nicky's Sunday Lunches have become the stuff of legend. We all became very close.

Having already developed an acute loathing for the local bus system, my need for transportation was stronger than ever. I had walked and taken the bus in and out of Bristol for a few weeks in full knowledge that it just wasn't a viable long-term solution. The bus was expensive and completely unreliable, often causing me to miss business meetings and the like.

So with no other ideas, I broke down and sent the word out to borrow a bicycle.

Another friend had an old 24-speed "hybrid" bike that wasn't being used and was roughly my size, so I bought myself a lock and a helmet and confirmed a pickup time. I'll never forget that first cycling trip from collecting my new wheels in-town to cycling the 7 miles back into Abbot's Leigh. Thankfully it wasn't raining, but the serious pain I was experiencing in my legs and back during the trip had me convinced I had made the wrong decision.

The following 6 weeks were a difficult time. With intermittent showers, expensive late buses and long walks, I had been fighting the pain of cycling in and out of Bristol. I had a hard time committing to the bicycle, despite the support of many of my cycling friends and the significant local cycling scene. But it was about to become non-optional.

One day while in-town, I received an email from a job recruiter who had found me through a colleague. He inquired about my availability for a 6-month contract 45 minutes north of Bristol, in the city of Gloucester.

During our first phone call I explained that I did not have a reliable means of transportation to consider any position so far from Bristol. I thanked him, exchanged the typical English pleasantries and hung up.

I had done in-house contracts before, but all locally. I had become accustomed to taking calls just like this one a few times each month.

Surprisingly, when he called back the next day, he said he had looked up the timetables and costs of a seasonal train ticket between Bristol and Gloucester and would be willing to add that plus some for travel time to my fees. We needed the money and craved the regularity of a monthly paycheck, and I accepted.

The only problem was that I was now living almost 8 miles from Bristol's Temple Meads train station and would have to get myself there for 7:30 each morning to catch my train, work for 8 hours, and then of course get back after dark. I accepted the contract and the fun began.

I cycled to Temple Meads every morning and back every evening for almost the entire contract, which had turned into 9 months. The timing of the train meant that my two bicycle trips were in the dark each day. It only took about two weeks for the ride to become easy. I went from walking about 6 miles per day to cycling at least 16 miles per day.

I lost probably 15 pounds of body fat in the first month, and I learned to love cycling. Physically and emotionally I felt superb. The unusually large leg muscles I inherited from my father had been previously built by years of skating, and were now revived. (Ruth loves to poke fun at my giant legs.)

Cycling had become my new way relieving stress while simultaneously solving my transportation, walking and energy issues and again, dramatically widening my range of exploration.

Just before the end of that work contract Ruth became pregnant with Titus. Two years had somehow flown by and we tearfully hugged Steve & Nicky before moving back home to Number 7. I completed the contract, thankful for the far shorter commute from our home in the city center over those last few weeks of work.

CYCLING AFFAIR

With my contract completed and being back at 7 Dalrymple Road, I dove straight back into nomadic working with a feverish desire.

I now had an entirely new and more efficient mode of transportation with which to recommence the tackling of my list, and I passionately marked my *Transportation* page 'complete'.

Contracting always gave us a strong leg-up financially, and we had done some major improvements to our home while living away at the mansion.

As in most areas of nomadic working, it didn't take long for me to begin strategizing about cycling. Now that I had a long-term proven interest in the sport, it was reasonable to consider buying my own bicycle.

To begin my new research, and to determine whether fixed-gear cycling was for me, I tried *never using other gears* on my borrowed bicycle. This experiment lasted for two weeks and was very enlightening; I loved that I didn't have to think about gears at all, and became convinced that the inherent mechanic simplicity of a fixed-gear bike was right up my alley. The additional physical challenge was also welcomed by then, but I had other requirements for a bicycle of my own as well.

I had just begun experimenting with traveling outside of Bristol by train to London, Bath or Cardiff for a day's work. I had 'mastered' Bristol and it was time to learn more by going further afield, but my borrowed bicycle was too heavy, ugly and embarrassing to bring with me on a train or bus. I needed a more *portable* bicycle so I could more easily explore.

I went online and began my research of a *fixed-gear folding bicycle*. Turns out that not a lot of manufacturers had considered my position, and the search quickly narrowed down to options I could count on a single hand. Two more were thrown out for price alone, which left the *Dahon Cadenza Solo* that I'd found online.

I began calling local bike shops to see if any stocked them and found Evans Bikes not too far away. I walked over with my printed webpage and price-matched a shiny new red-on-white fixed-gear folding bike, and gladly returned my trusty old loaner.

I used that new Dahon bike to death. I folded it up with me onto buses and trains. It saw action on the streets of Bath, Cardiff and London and even Los Angeles, where it played a key role in breaking my left collarbone.

I learned a lot about bicycles; how to fix a flat, change a tire, replace brakes and after the collarbone incident, how to cycle safely and tune my brakes. The mechanics of bicycles had become a hobby, and much to Ruth's dismay, I set up a makeshift shop in the conservatory at home where I could tinker a little more.

After a year of hard riding, I had assembled my first homemade bicycle from loose parts off Ebay, friends, Amazon and a local bike charity The Bristol Bike Project.

I now had a sweet, unique fixed-gear bike that I loved riding. It was light, compact and nimble—perfect for the city traffic in Bristol, through which I was now whipping with confidence.

I kept the Dahon for awhile because it folded, but eventually my classic sensibilities assisted in the decision to only keep my new 'Frankenstein' build, and the Dahon was sold.

I treated my subsequent workdays outside the city as 'slow days' where I would walk and take in the sights between work sessions, and this ended up suiting me just fine. But a couple times I brought the Frankenstein with me on the train to London and enjoyed the freedom it offered to explore more of London's streets.

(I ended up busting that sweet little Italian steel frame, and scavenged the parts for the *Frankenstein v2*, which is still my daily-driver today because I built it like a tank! ;-)

In the coming years I would dive deep into Bristol's cycling and fixed-gear scenes. I started an online directory to help other newbies get involved, which quickly resulted in requests coming from other cities for their own local directories. I got to know all the key players in the local scenes and wider into London, Manchester, Newcastle, Bath, Leeds and Cardiff and co-sponsored a Bike Polo competition in London. (Yes, bike polo is a real sport, with athletes, jerseys, teams, tournaments and everything!)

Though my two primary modes of transportation were walking and cycling, I eventually considered that a car or truck could be an even larger step in nomadic working.

I don't want to give off the impression of being a glutton for punishment… I like to sleep in or enjoy the controlled temperature of a car just as much as the next person. I connected to cycling so much because cycling was so 'connected' to the environment I wanted to experience, and my other options were limited.

Cars don't offer that same connectedness, but they do have their fair share of unique abilities which are just as suitable for nomadic working as a bicycle (or kayak, for that matter).

I learned that *it's not really important what mode of transportation you use.* The important thing about nomadic working is that in everything you do, you strive to improve your experience. Cars can do that just as well as a bicycle, but in different ways which are just as valid.

But even today, you'd have to pry my bike from my cold, dead hands. And with that, let's get back to the story shall we?

I'd caught the cycling bug and wasn't looking back. My initial foray into cycling was full of challenges, but had resulted in a lifelong love affair with the bicycle. I've since built other bikes and my knowledge has grown. But it wouldn't be the end of my *transportation* list-item because after all, I had brought a love for cars with me from California that remained unfulfilled.

With the bicycle having dramatically increased my available range of distance, a new, more immediate problem had become apparent.

ROUTE PLANNING

I had become very comfortable on my bicycle. I loved cycling so much that I took every opportunity to do so, sometimes crossing the entire City of Bristol just to spend a little more time with the wind in my hair and the sights of the city. It didn't take long before I had physically exhausted myself by covering sometimes 40 miles in a day within the city limits. While distances like that were typical for many of my friends, I wasn't in that good of shape!

I allowed myself the luxury of enjoying my new mode of transportation for about a month before diving into my new list item, *Route optimization.*

Before heading out for the day, I took a moment to think about where I wanted to work, how much time I had *to just explore,* and locations I knew I wanted to try. This usually didn't take more than 30 seconds on the way out the door, but sometimes I'd find my resulting route a little stale and open up my list of new locations to get some fresh ideas.

That simple strategy seemed to work well enough, and it started building new little habits in my day. I'd arrive first thing in the morning at a location I'd been wanting to explore, and by the time I had exhausted my productivity there, I'd find a great lunch place next door, or look across the river to find a quaint little park area overlooking the water.

It turned out that slowing down a bit was opening my eyes to a finer-grain of detail, and my list of locations started growing far more quickly, and becoming more detailed.

At first, they looked like *City Park* being scrawled across my notebook, but turned into a list of notes like *that tree stump with graffiti on it 2.3 miles down the bike path on the South side toward Bath City.*

I'd built a habit of thinking ahead—something which never came naturally to me almost regardless of subject. I had a chronology of locations in my head before I even mounted my bicycle that morning. I had a rough idea of the timing in which I'd exhaust a stretch of productivity, and when I'd be hungry or need a break. If I had some extra time I'd cycle the 17 miles into Bath City and work there for the day, with a whole new urban center to explore. If I was really busy with work, I'd keep the routes short and direct between locations.

I became pretty good at preparing for inclement weather, and my fear of being caught in the rain decreased as I learned more about being prepared for it. I also learned to "read the weather" more effectively, which let me time my cycling trips accordingly. But if I did get caught in the rain, I was prepared for it.

Route-planning became almost a thoughtless habit that was now second-nature throughout the day, and I looked forward to times when I could get a long trip on my bike to explore an entirely new area, or when I could just hunker-down and write for a couple hours at one of my favorite quiet places.

This newfound freedom that the bicycle offered made me feel so much more free to explore. I was spending far less time traveling than I had been before, and covering more distance. It allowed me to make more stops that were farther away. I could take more time to relax in more beautiful locations.

That, in-turn, inspired more creativity in my normal design work. The way I had leveraged the bicycle was having a tangible impact on my life. Less work and more fun with the same or better amount of productivity. #win

STRATEGY
EVOLVING

I had developed a rhythm, and with work steadily coming in, I had
a reasonable budget with which I could begin tackling some of the
larger issues that plagued my daily anti-routines.

I attacked them with a vengeance. *Identify, research,
experiment, apply.* I had prioritized items on my list by *severity of
need,* and strategically researched each possibility before making
a purchase.

Not all the problems were solved by simply buying something, but
many of them were. I don't mean to make it sound easy; buying
stuff doesn't always have perfect long-term results.

Whatever pack I was using seemed to lack something I needed.
I made several purchases of different messenger bags and
backpacks over the years in search of perfection. Eventually I
settled on a couple key players whom had proven themselves over
time. These were a black backpack by Incase and a black TPU-lined
messenger bag by The North Face... but even they had their share
of downsides.

After years of experimenting with different bags, I recently settled
on the "Carrerita" by Crafted Goods—a small manufacturer out
of Bogotá. It's a small messenger bag that is a great all-rounder. It

covers all of my needs quite nicely... but back to the story.

A few items proved to be difficult in this way... items which could only be researched to a degree before actual trials were necessary. Items that fit into this category were gloves, jackets, base layers and eventually shoes made their way in, too, as I had more of a need to be presentable in business meetings.

I began amassing a considerable collection of shoes and bags, and Ruth expressed how much she missed the extra space in the wardrobe. Looking back, I wish I had been even more scrutinizing with my purchases.

Business had a way of throwing wrenches into the cogs of my systems. Contract work often called for slightly nicer attire, which made travel by bicycle difficult. I tried packing a spare change of clothes, cycling slower as to not sweat, and even packing cologne with me or showering at the office.

I had spent this entire journey so far never really needing to look particularly fancy—many clients were friends who didn't care, and others had been busy in an office somewhere far away. But as my client base grew upward, the need to be presentable followed suit.

In those days clothing brands like Timberland, Patagonia and The North Face were just beginning to think about this problem of *cycling to work,* and there wasn't a lot on the market. Most specialty items that were available online from companies like Outlier and Rapha proved to be priced well out of my budget. I had to be creative if I was going to address this one effectively.

Most issues of nomadic working are easily addressed by little more than a bit of critical thought. But there are the rare few that can literally take years. For me, a daily bag and transportation fit into that category of *actually, this isn't easy*.

But they also tend to be the ones which pay off the most—my obsession with bags has actually been fulfilled. My trial-and-error with so many different methods of transportation resulted in my cycling hobby—something that's now a significant part of my life. It's not all easy, and it's not like nomadic working is *the thing* that's surfacing these problems—they're things that would be there anyway.

So let's explore that a little bit. I'll start by talking about researching products, buying stuff, and how it wasn't really any different for me than it would be for anyone else.

NORMAL LIFE

I couldn't afford to just go to the local outdoor gear store and spend a thousand pounds on whatever I wanted to test. All of this happened in-sync with normal life, which is why my experiments with things I already owned outnumbered my new purchases by roughly four-to-one.

For new items I had researched and wanted to test, I added them to my birthday and Christmas lists. If I had a bit of extra money, I'd go out and buy the most promising items on my lists every now-and-then. But like most, I was always limited to a budget. I spent far more time testing new rules and experimenting with new strategies than I did shopping. Over years this was slow, but effective, and now I know that was a good thing.

The few times that I did get a bit of extra money would often result in me splitting my attention between too many things at-once, and therefore not be able to fully focus on one, two or three things. I remember finishing a 6-month work contract in 2008. Ruth and I had, by then, focused on strategically paying off bills, improving the house and putting some money away for a rainy day. When the contract ended we thought well, that was useful. We had accomplished a lot in the time and felt happy with ourselves for budgeting. And then a final paycheck came through a month afterwards that we weren't expecting.

The money was just 'extra', so Ruth and I put a little in savings and then split the rest and went shopping.

Ruth bought a nice pair of boots and a jacket from Joules. I bought the slimmed-down version of the Incase backpack I already had, a set of micro-fleece thermals, a pair of nice Sony headphones and a new iPhone. These were all things I 'kinda wanted', but they weren't researched—this shopping trip was just supposed to be *fun*.

As I enjoyed all this new 'stuff' the following week, it disrupted my usual flow of focus on the few, small items that were 'current' in my notebook. It slowed my normal pace of strategy and experimentation. This is the kind of 'normal life' events I keep referring to. In terms of strategy, I counted it as a distraction. Eventually I caught up, but it was difficult with my attention being pulled in so many directions. That's why I prefer nowadays to focus on one or two things at a time until they're resolved, and then move on.

The 'net' effect that nomadic working had on normal life was positive. If I could have done more in less time, I would have, but just like you I was subject to my circumstances, and I was happy to be integrating all of my learning into our lifestyle, and at our lifestyle's natural pace (most of the time). Though I was always eager to move down my list, I felt like my normal pace was easily manageable.

It's not like every December I'd sit Ruth down, stand on a podium and announce *"Okaaay, Christmas Lists. Let's consult the Nomadic Working Bible and see what it says..."* I couldn't have gotten away with something like that anyway ;-) but I never wanted to. I liked that it was all quite transparent.

IT'S A THING

Socially, I didn't really want the whole thing to become a big
focus of attention to anyone else—the strategies and challenges
were plenty to keep me busy without bothering others with it.
I went about my day seeing friends, family, clients and colleagues
and operated like a reasonably normal human being, as far as I
could tell.

I never desired to be 'that guy' clad in neon lycra because it reduced
wind resistance on his bicycle, or so that others might look in
admiration at what I was doing. I was enjoying my work, life,
friends and new family, and all this was just a part of my personal
daily routine, rarely to be shared with anyone. Really, it ended
up being quite a private thing, but not because I consciously
kept it secret—it just never occurred to me that anyone might
be interested.

Though I was happy enough with how it was all so transparent, it
had become a large enough part of my life that it eventually started
popping up above the surface of social interactions, like the tip
of an iceberg. I'd have a friend ask me about "remote working" or
"how the heck do you *not* have an office?" People noticed that every
time they saw me at the park, I was working. Or if I bumped into
someone at the pub, they'd learned to ask whether I was working.

By this time, the term *remote working* had made a few small
appearances, and with more years under my belt I was more widely

familiar with trends in the creative industries. I became conscious that what I had been doing was very unusual indeed, and did not fit the description of remote working, but was so much more. I'm sure I wasn't the only one, but I was certainly the only one in my personal sphere, wider professional circles, and even within the wider creative industry that I knew of who was working daily without an office and in different places.

I had a few designer friends ask me about freelancing and working remotely. Each time I would say that remote working was very rewarding and that I enjoyed the freedom, but that running one's own business was an entirely different affair that required far more focus.

It never occurred to me to call it anything other than *remote working* because it would have required some explanation while the new, trendy term was becoming more widely understood. I had no need for others to know the exact nature of my lifestyle, and how it differed from remote working. I never bothered actively speaking about it with anyone before launching nomadicworking.com

On the odd occasion that someone would ask what I do, I would simply say *I'm a designer.* If they asked about where I worked, I would reply with something like *oh, here and there.* I assumed no one really cared, and I was probably right. They weren't the people who might have cared, you and I are.

I remember once sitting at The Watershed in Bristol as I thought to myself *"The only thing that makes me a remote worker is the fact that I'm not in a central office. What I'm doing isn't really remote working. It's something else. I'm constantly on-the-move, and*

*doing that on-purpose because it inspires creativity and improves
my lifestyle. What I'm doing is* nomadic, *not just remote."*

I wouldn't consider the term *nomadic working* until I left England,
but that day at The Watershed, it was on the tip of my tongue.
Of course, the term doesn't really matter. I settled on it for my
website because it's clear, simple, descriptive (and the domain was
available). I was too busy enjoying the *doing* of it to care about
what I should call it back then. I still believed I was alone in it all.

A few years into it I started writing a detailed how-to book
about the ins-and-outs of remote working. I wrote about 25,000
words before realizing that *remote* working is not the same as
nomadic working.

Most remote workers use an office of some sort, and all my
findings about wifi, travel etc. were useless to them. The vast
majority of remote workers I know personally all work from home.
So I stopped writing as I pondered the question *who will benefit
from this kind of unusual information?*

MANAGING UNFORESEENS

Since my 8-hour days at Starbucks I knew that life had a way of sporadically throwing wrenches in the cogs of my well-oiled anti-routines.

I'd bump into friends who'd sit down for an hour-long discussion, Ruth might call with some family emergency, my bike would get a flat or my phone would be stolen. I had simple phone calls turn into 3-hour conferences, rain frying my electronics, and a few serious spills off my bicycle. Several times, due to the nature of running a small design business, I just went flat broke.

Sometimes you can only be *so* prepared. Things just stop whatever you're doing and there's nothing you can do about it. Some of these interruptions were delightful impromptu chats over coffee with a friend, and other times they spelled the end of my workday to be replaced with a frantic rest of the evening. It's just life.

As usual, I dealt as well as I could with each of them. I learned to fix a flat tire in 10 minutes wherever I was and started carrying spare tubes. I learned to politely inform friends that I didn't have time to chat at that particular point. (When people see you sitting at a cafe with your computer they assume you're just relaxing, and that it's fair game.)

A few times when I ran out of money I'd make coffee at home and put it into my insulated mug, pack a lunch and snacks and just stay outdoors all day. In short, I did the best I could with what I had. But the nature of being a nomadic worker is this: *you're outside your comfort zone much of the time, and often that's on-purpose, because change is inspirational and exploration enriches life.*

"The Unforeseens" are an inevitable side-effect of working nomadically. *Outside your comfort zone* is a bit of an understatement; it's probably clearer to say that you're consciously moving between environments that are, in most ways, *purposefully* outside of your control. Every strange thing that can happen probably will. That's kind of the glass-half-empty version of it, but true nonetheless.

Is it worth it? Every. Single. Bit.

Like a marriage or having children or so many other things worth doing, nomadic working yields a harvest that is greater than the sum of its parts. You get more out than what you put in, from day one, and that's why I've never stopped. It really is about one's comfort zone, and that is perhaps the biggest challenge of nomadic working as a whole – you've got to become the Zen master of getting outside your comfort zone – because if there's one thing that nomadic working is *not*, it's *stationary*.

I was making much effort to deal with the rain, transportation that would 'connect' me to my environment, and all of the other unforeseens that came along with it.

Why not just cobble together a home office, or get a desk job where the building is temperature-controlled? Because in my experience it was very rare to find inspiration and a sense of adventure that endured there, and I wasn't willing to let such a huge part of my life be void of those two things.

You've heard the term *adrenaline junky,* and I'd say there's some truth to that when it comes to nomadic working. Once you've tasted what it offers, it's very difficult to go back. I probably should have printed that on the cover ;-)

LIFESTYLE

What hooked me about nomadic working – well before I knew what I was doing – was the inspiration. I rarely wanted for any creative inspiration—I was experiencing new people, places and things every day.

Nomadic working is such a rich lifestyle. Have you ever moved away from a place where you had spent many years and said *"I can't believe I never did that, or went there."* I have. When I moved from California to England, my general understanding of geography completely changed and I found myself saying *I can't believe I never saw The Grand Canyon, it was only six hours away.*

Many, many things were on that list when I left California. *I should have visited San Francisco more often. I should have seen Carlsbad Caverns. I should have hiked more. I should have seen Napa Valley. I should have gone further up the Pacific Crest Trail.* My list grew with each year in England.

While nomadic working doesn't necessarily mean more opportunities for family vacations, it certainly means more freedom for travel and exploration—whether the family comes or not. Had I been doing this in California, I could have taken a 3-day trip to The Grand Canyon and worked in that beautiful scene the whole time. I could have setup shop inside Carlsbad Caverns for the day, because nothing was stopping me.

And that's precisely what I was doing now. One day I worked in the park outside Buckingham Palace in London. Another day I setup right on the beautiful River Avon that runs through Bristol, with the Clifton Suspension Bridge overlooking the Avon Gorge, where the pirate Blackbeard once sailed.

Once I rode my bicycle to Portishead to work from a quaint little café as the icy water splashed on the rocks beside the pier. Another time, while at an arts retreat, I worked at a bench for a few hours just north of the white cliffs of Dover, with the shores of France just visible in the distance.

During an arts conference in the Austrian Alps, I setup at a table on the northwest turret of the castle in which I was staying, overlooking the beautiful snow-covered valley of Mittersill before me. The next day, I hiked across the valley and up the adjacent mountain to work at a little artistically-crafted wooden shack which I just happened upon.

Once in Paris I left our flat and worked at a Parisienne café around the corner with the romantic nightlife of Paris all around me, and the Eiffel Tower sparkling in the distance. To-date, I've worked in Granada, London, Salzburg, Paris, Dublin, Bray, Munich, Vienna, Cardiff, Portishead, Los Angeles, New York City, San Francisco, Stockholm, Barcelona, Glasgow, Dundee, Thailand and countless lesser-known places as I traveled. Because *why not?*

Cutting the office cord had tipped the scale of so many things that would make my life more rich with experience, people and general happiness. I wasn't going to give this up for anything. It was in my blood.

A FRENCH
SNOW MASS

With a new work contract on the horizon and no convenient train in-between, I began researching cars for sale that would suit my needs, plus ideally go a little beyond them. But before I go on, let me tell you the story that resulted in me wanting *a particular kind* of car.

My brother-in-law had purchased a little chalet in the South of France, and he offered it to us over Christmas. With no other plans, we gratefully accepted and began making arrangements.

We were to fly into Bezíer Airport just north of the Cevénne National Forest in which the chalet was located about 2 hours south, where Ruth and I would enjoy a quiet French Christmas together.

Upon arrival in Bezíer, we located the car which he had kept at the airport specifically for this journey. It was an 80's Mercedes diesel estate wagon in bronze. Though it had apparently seen better days, I fired it up and we headed to the nearest grocery store to stock up for the holiday.

Shortly after having loaded food into the back of the nearly 2-ton rear-wheel-drive wagon, snow began to lightly fall, and the motorway slowed to a crawl. But with a full tank of diesel, gobs of holiday spirit and all the time in the world, we happily carried on.

After 3 hours on the motorway we hadn't even reached our halfway point. The GPS unit that lived in the car needed constant adjusting to maintain a charge and our patience began to wane. It was dark and the snow intensified.

After almost 5 hours we finally turned onto our exit ramp for the rest of the journey through the winding mountainous roads of the Cevénne. *Thank God* we thought.

Cold, exhausted and fed up, we followed the GPS around unpaved, narrow cliff-side paths. The brush grew thicker and the roads less maintained the further we went. Not having seen any signs of life for over an hour, we rounded a sharp corner to find that the. snowplow had apparently turned around at this point, as evinced by the ten-foot wall of snow across the road before us.

To the left was the mountain, and to the right a steep cliff. We had no choice but to turn around and find another way. That was about the time we realized we had nearly exhausted our fuel supply.

Having found an alternate route we carried on back down the mountain. We were worried about the tank running dry in the middle of nowhere in the 15°F weather with no town on the GPS within 20 miles, and with the snow showing no signs of letting up.

Suddenly we turned a corner that was sharper than I had anticipated and slid into a snow embankment. The car was high-centered and the passenger side almost buried in the snow mass.

After calming the panic that had set in, Ruth and I exited the car and began digging it out with magazines and anything else we could find. We would coax the car forward, then backward, then dig some more.

After about 20 minutes of this, we finally freed it. Frozen to our bones, we hopped into the slightly warmer cabin and had started reversing out when a dark object in the snow caught my eye. It was my passport. It had slipped out of my pocket while digging and was half-buried in the snow. I got out and retrieved it before we restarted our difficult journey. *Phew.*

We warmed up a little and got back to discussing what we might do when we ran out of fuel before reaching our destination. By now it was almost midnight, and we knew that no gas stations would be open, even if we could find one or make it there.

We continued down the mountain until we found our alternate route, which to our surprise led us through a tiny village with a single-pump gas station. The only sign of life was a skinny stray dog running through the snow. Orange street lamps lit the 4 or 5 structures that made up the village.

With the tiniest bit of hope, we pulled into the station that had clearly been shut for hours as the snow fell around us. It was well past midnight.

I rapped on the window furiously for what seemed like 10 minutes. With all hope lost, I turned away to look around for some lodge or chalet that might take us in at this late hour, and the thought of leaving the only civilization we had seen since leaving Bezíer was too much to bear.

While walking back to the car, I saw Ruth frantically pointing behind me toward the window of the station. A middle-aged Frenchman had awoken and was at the window. He opened it and in the worst French, I attempted to explain our situation.

He noted that the snow had taken out the phone lines, which meant that our cards would not work, and that he could only take cash. We gathered every Euro note and coin we could find, which only amounted to maybe a quarter tank. He accepted my constant thanks and apologies. I pumped the diesel and we were back on the road.

Not more than an hour later we arrived in *Florac*—the village in which our chalet resided. Whether due to the emotion of relief or actual reality, it was one of the most adorable and quaint places I had ever seen—even at night and in our state of exhaustion.

We had been instructed to collect the chalet key from "the video store guy". The problem was, it was so late at night. The only sign of activity tumbled out of a single door in front of the only local bar. We parked the car out front and entered.

Just *seeing other humans who were in good spirits* seemed to lift our own, and after having attempted conversations with many locals in-search of *video guy*, we found someone who knew him, spoke a little English and was willing to help. The girl motioned for us to follow her outside.

After a short walk through the snow on a silent cobblestone road we arrived at video guy's front door. To our surprise, she banged hard and yelled up at the window, but to no avail. In the frozen darkness, we slipped down the cobblestone path back to the bar.

We ordered some hot drinks and sat in silence. We had no other option but to sleep in the car. As we finished our drinks, we got up to put our coats and hats back on when a young man in his late-twenties approached us. His name was Tom and he seemed kind. In broken English he replied to our story... *"I am watching a house not too far away. Come and sleep there tonight and tomorrow you can come back to Florac to get your key."*

With no other choice, we gladly accepted. We followed Tom to a house in mid-renovation outside of town, and suddenly it became clear that he was a worker who had been contracted to improve the house while its owners were away.

It was a work-site for sure, but some semblance of bedrooms still existed. He filled an empty 2-liter Coke bottle with boiled water from a kettle and handed it to Ruth before showing us to a nearby bedroom with a bed and linens.

At first I didn't know what the Coke bottle was for, and thought it was a strange thing to do or some strange French way of flirting with Ruth. Soon I realized it's incredible ability to warm an entire bed with two inhabitants (me and Ruth—thank you very much), and we slept deeply.

The next morning we thanked Tom and returned to Florac. We found video guy and entered our chalet with his key. The interior seemed colder than outside, and after unloading all of the (now frozen) food from the Mercedes, we started loading the wood-burning stoves with logs and kindling.

We gathered blankets and sat on the sofa directly in front of the stove and truly warmed up to our cores for the first time in what seemed like days. But we knew we couldn't sit there forever.

Over the next three days we fought the 3 stoves in the house, trying to make at least a dent in the temperature, to no avail. We took a couple walks around town to warm up and had a couple meals out, but the town was quiet just before Christmas and most places had closed for the season.

Not being able to warm that little house in Florac, and with no other means than setting the whole thing aflame (does frozen wood burn?), we decided to return home early to try and catch Christmas morning in Bristol.

We packed and locked up with a sentiment of *good riddance* and drove back to Bezíer for our flight home, and this is where I pickup the story about the first car I bought in England.

(Now, when Ruth or myself comes home after a hard day we say *"I had such a Florac of a day."*)

NEW WHEELS

Having completed some research for a reliable, *four-wheel-drive* car within my budget of £550 (about $1,000 USD back then), I found a silver 1995 Subaru Legacy sedan for £430 from a local farmer. God only knows how he got mud caked on all three axes of the interior. I was ecstatic as I drove it off the farm and back home.

With only 60,000 miles on the clock, this was the steal of the century, and she was running great. I was glad to be prepared for this upcoming work contract, as well as any weather that could be thrown our way with the Subaru's four-wheel-drive and reliable 2.2-liter 4-cylinder engine. I had always wanted a Subaru—I think they struck me as *utilitarian* or something. They just spoke my language.

What I didn't expect was how strongly my love for cars would be rekindled by this stout little machine. The trip to Florac and back had taught me that cars were more than just transportation, but that if a good choice was made, they could be the only thing that gets you through a life-or-death situation. From then on I would always think about cars as so much more than a fashion choice, or just a way to get across town.

Suddenly the fancy Infiniti G35 I had loved so dearly back in Pomona seemed like the automotive equivalent of a hog in a bow-tie (thanks for that one, Dad). That old Mercedes had barely managed to get us through France, and I vowed to never let myself or my family be in that situation again.

This little Subaru would have climbed out of that French snow mass like a mountain goat. Now I considered cars *a tool by which to accomplish a wide range of potentially life-threatening tasks.*

I was at the tail end of my 9-month contract when we got the car. It ended up being a very welcome break from cycling in the snow.

The little Subaru was perfect for the task of commuting the 45-minute drive in frequently bad weather which had begun worsening as we got further into winter—and this winter would be the most white and cold I would ever see during my 7 years in England.

The little conservatory I had re-purposed as my bike shop started double-duty for both cars and bikes. I started on the basics. First thing was to clean all the mud from the interior which proved a laborious task, but soon it was done and I was shocked at how great it all came out.

There was little sign of wear except for lines starting on the driver's seat bolster. With everything clean, I conditioned the gray leather seats and scrubbed spots from the carpet. I replaced all the consumables; brake pads and rotors, filters and fluids and eventually tires.

I signed up to an online forum of Subaru Legacy owners which unexpectedly broadened my horizons. There were hundreds of other people in England with the same car, and with even more enthusiasm than I, and so many projects came from ideas found on that forum.

I sourced used Japanese Domestic Market (JDM) parts which were nicer than what had been imported to England in 1995.

I replaced the headlights, front and rear bumpers, hood, wheels and even power-folding wing mirrors with JDM equivalents, which I wired up to the JDM switch to make them work.

I rebuilt the starter motor and cleaned the block. I clayed, waxed and polished the paint and she was looking amazing. All of this work was done either on our conservatory bench or in the street of our cul-de-sac at Number 7.

I had tinkered with cars back in California, but this was a whole new level of *learning and doing* for me. I was hooked, and happy to learn that I had made a 'Subaru-buddy' at my new work contract who was much further-along than I.

Rich had a 2002 Subaru Forester XT, a turbo model that was very fast. While mine was a non-turbo model, it had the widely-coveted 2.2-liter 4-cylinder "boxer" engine, which had a reputation for being the most reliable Subaru engine ever made, and that fact made me happy. The capability of its four-wheel-drive combined with the luxury of the interior leather and very nice exterior lines made me want for nothing, even #MoarSpeed.

DRIVING ROUTINE

With my contract coming to an end, the Subaru had never let me down and I was looking forward to finding out how it could become a part of my working lifestyle.

I left the contract's office for the last time and drove back to Bristol. The next morning I drove the car to Park Street and set myself up at Goldbrick House for a special planning session, fancy coffee in-hand.

My first thought was about *routine;* how would I deal with Bristol's crazy traffic, roads and parking? I decided that my first trial would be to simply drive to a particular central location in the morning, walk short distances during the day and then drive back at night.

I did so that day and the next, and eventually started mixing that with cycling and leaving the car at home. Ruth and I took road trips to Cardiff and visited family in Wales in the comfort and reliability of the Subaru.

We could now go wherever we wanted, whenever we wanted, and the newfound freedom improved our options in life and in work.

I remember re-learning a lot of the practicalities of owning and operating a car in England versus in California. Insurance and fuel was so much more expensive here in England.

My wimpy little 2.2-liter 4-cylinder engine was considered by the British to be a gas-guzzling hot-rod. But to me, it was the least powerful car I had ever owned to-date, and only relented to a four-banger because of the gas prices and my budget.

While I had the Subaru I made a few trips to London for a work day or two, but I never really got an opportunity to do a proper working road trip, though I wanted to. I always loved road trips, especially when I got to plan and execute them, and this became a deep desire that wouldn't be fulfilled for years.

But right now we had more important things in-mind, namely the birth of our son Titus.

A FAMILY
ADDITION

Ruth and I are both very independent people. We've both had
to carve out our own paths, and neither of us have really done
things 'normally'.

In her earlier school years, she joined her school's debate team who
flew to New Zealand to win the debating championships there.
Her penchant for passionate communication helped her become a
frequent and key speaker at the church – and many other churches
and conferences across the UK and abroad – which was the
circumstance when we first met in California.

Having grown up in West Wales, Ruth eventually followed her
sister Rachel to Bristol when she was just 17 and having recently
finished her required school years. Upon arrival in Bristol she
enrolled at Bristol UWE and completed her History degree.

She eventually found her calling at the church Rachel had invited
her to, and Ruth dug her heels into church work, eventually
becoming the Associate Pastor of the church after years of
volunteering and working other related jobs.

With Ruth having come full-term, we welcomed a heavy and
healthy baby boy into our arms on November 13, 2010 at the
hospital in Bristol. Titus' arrival meant we now had three different

nationalities in the family: American, Welsh and English. We brought Titus home to his room that we'd enjoyed preparing and it hit us that *we're now a fully-fledged family.*

Titus forever changed how Ruth and I 'dreamed & schemed' together. We found ourselves discussing his future and the various ways in which we could secure it.

We talked about parenting styles and discussed our own upbringings. Having an entire human under our sole care & responsibility made Ruth and I change the way we considered our personal goals. It had the overall effect of simply broadening our horizons.

Our world became bigger, and somehow simultaneously smaller as we focused on 'the family' more, and I enjoyed having this greater purpose in life.

HOME OFFICE

As Ruth and I settled into parenthood, our routines were forced to change around raising the baby. We both adjusted our schedules heavily to give each other breaks and 'time out'. As always, nomadic working flowed around these changes; the biggest of which was that it became more difficult for me to be away from home for a solid 8-hour stretch each day.

With sleep being pretty much a thing of the past, my energy levels were at an all-time low, as were Ruth's. We quickly learned that it wasn't realistic to do the 'single-income family' thing in the sense that *one person works while the other raises the children.*

The more we thought about it, the more we realized *that wasn't what we wanted anyway.* I wanted more time with the kids (as far as my Ricky-Bobby Syndrome would allow) and Ruth wanted more time to get back into her work. So we started getting creative.

By it's simplest definition, nomadic working, I suppose, is *working without an office.* But at this point for us, setting up a home office was exactly what we needed. It would provide a way for me to work between this new, more complex schedule of raising a child, but it would also serve as a fall-back option when my energy levels were too low to be running around town all day.

So I began. I purchased a little table from the 'bargain basement' at IKEA and setup a small, simple desk that would be out of the way when not in use, but nice enough for me to be productive when I did use it. I decorated it with my small vinyl figure collection and enjoyed having my own private little corner in the house. I worked there sporadically for a couple years, but even having this little space exactly how I wanted it couldn't keep me from getting out.

I learned that having a home office is a good thing, and I would try to keep one from now on, in the off-chance that I needed it. Having a home office has become just another 'site' for me to work from. Even though I rarely use it, it's really nice to have it as a fall-back option.

(Now that we're in Fort Collins, Colorado, my home-office came in handy when I was just learning how to deal with the freezing temperatures of the Colorado winter. I would use it for an hour or so, and then go out to try some of my ideas for nomadic working.)

DIGITAL
OPTIMIZATION

In my line of work it's essential that you are able to work seamlessly with other developers, designers and managers. When you couple that with nomadic working, it becomes even more important because – though you're rarely in the office – things still need to run smoothly.

I had, over the years, experimented with various ways to streamline and organize my design work and my business:

Web software like DropBox, PivotalTracker, Asana, Google Apps, Evernote, Trello, InVision, Basecamp, GitHub and others made it possible for me to collaborate seamlessly and avoid the mess of emails, CDs and USB drives. I could share design files, leave notes, collaboratively edit copy and even manage my billing easily, and digitally, from anywhere.

Without simple tools like these, running a design business without an office would have been twice as difficult—which was my experience when I first started. I constantly tried new services, and as time went on, more options became available.

When you work in a digital field, you realize how crucial it is to use the right software. Before I had signed up to Freshbooks I was spending too much time manually creating and issuing invoices. That simple software cut that time to a fraction of what it had been. Like many other services I used, they always came in handy for the time I needed them.

When you're out on the road all day, every day, organization is paramount, and digital organization proved to be just as important as planning ahead and organizing my bag for the day, or planning my daily route in the morning.

I usually had an average of 3 different projects on at a time. Each one had it's own set of preferred services for digital organization and collaboration. In time, the fact that *I had learned to use so many of them* became another reason for clients to choose me over my competitors for their projects.

Learning to work within their systems just improved my own knowledge. Many of the services I use today, like DropBox, were introduced to me by a client who preferred that I use the same systems as they did.

Integrating the knowledge of these services into my own workflow freed up more time in nomadic working and helped me to stay well-organized. In today's increasingly digital world, workers in this field can no longer afford to focus solely on the physical.

Fast-forwarding to today, these kinds of web-based services have made digital management and collaboration almost entirely seamless. Being a designer, I use an Apple laptop, iPhone and an iPad. Apple's iCloud service seamlessly syncs all my notes, email, contacts and calendars across devices without me ever thinking about it.

It sounds silly now, but it was a huge pain-in-the-butt 10 years ago. (Anyone remember ActiveSync or Palm?)

I continue to use DropBox, PivotalTracker, GitHub and Google Drive today, and they've become an integral part of my workflow—without which I would be spending far too much time in digital management. I love that I can delegate these tasks to reliable services, and free up my mental space for nomadic working. After all, digital organization is just another tool available to design one's work/life.

ENGLAND ≠ CALIFORNIA

Now that I had been settled in England, doing everything the English way, it became apparent that things were very different from California. The shiny newness of Bristol had long since worn off, and my small criticisms grew into large problems.

Suddenly I realized how the simplest things were so much more difficult to accomplish here. I had grown up in a state which had largely been built in the wake of the passing industrial revolution.

Streets were wide; designed for motorized vehicles. If a house aged past 60 years, most of the time it was simply torn down and rebuilt. If a business wasn't being competitive, the market demanded it be replaced by a more lucrative, efficient and consumer-friendly version.

By comparison, England was a country that had slowly been adapting to the 21st century after a millennium in the dark ages— and only where space and industry allowed it to happen easily.

Streets in Bristol are narrow and busy, parking virtually non-existent, private businesses often slow and self-centered, and the frequently terrible weather seemed to amplify these shortcomings that manifested themselves in many aspects of daily life, turning what should have been simple tasks into demanding ordeals. For example, getting groceries:

In California, the need for this task at all was far less pronounced. With abundant cheap and healthy food on many street corners of Orange County, many residents could afford to eat out for breakfast and lunch, and often dinner.

When one needed food at home, it was a case of *stepping out the door into the sun and proceeding directly into the reasonably nice car.* You drive around the corner to the supermarket and saunter down aisles of fantastic selections (which are subsidized by decades of local farming industry deals and cheap international trade), checkout and leave the cart in the parking lot (because it's someone full-time job to return it for you).

You then drive home through the wide, efficient roads to park outside your front door (it's still sunny) and the worst part – bring the food inside with your own two hands (a task I expect to be subsidized eventually). In England, for me anyway, that task looked liked this:

Check the weather. Rain again. Shocker. Bundle up and start walking. Avoid the drug deal happening on the sidewalk ahead by crossing the street. Watch out for that cyclist dodging the car who's trying to park on top of our sidewalk. Walk around the car and avoid eye-contact with the dodgy fellow exiting. Oh dear what was that!? Some kid on a BMX just grabbed my mobile phone and rode off. Cross seven more streets, dodge three more cyclists. I just stepped in a puddle and soaked my shoe and sock. Decline an offer for drugs. Is my wallet still there? Oh look, there's the grocery store. Step over the homeless person at the door and arrive inside.

My phone is ringing, but I cant be bothered to take off my gloves to answer it. Load up the trolley which is not allowed outside the store, but don't buy so much that we can't carry it home. Get that smaller jug of milk, over there. Damn—the extortionately priced car insurance just came out, so we'll have to come back for the rest next time we're paid. Repeat the journey in-reverse order. Arrive home to change clothes, warm the house and make tea. We're exhausted.

Oh yeah, the food goes in the fridge, but it won't all fit. No matter, just put it out back because it's probably colder outside than in the fridge. #MoarTea

For me, circumstances like this were my personal reality that could never be understood by those around me because my Californian point-of-reference came from 6,000 miles away.

I grew frustrated and indignant on an increasingly regular basis, and it became so pronounced in my life that I complained to Ruth about it, which she somehow endured.

The frequent difficulty of what I expected to be *simple tasks* nagged at me, and inevitably affected the way I worked as well. It seemed like I was becoming frustrated at one thing or another all the time. Settling into the ways of English life was not a task I had expected to be so difficult.

(I've painted this picture in an exaggerated way in order to show how I felt, rather than 100% reality. I'm expressing the gaping chasm between my two worlds as I perceived it at the time, but the charm of England would always win me over.)

GIVING UP

With the difficulties of life in England becoming more than I could bear, I decided that *working without an office* was too big a task to maintain since it made up for such a huge portion of my daily life. My productivity was not where I wanted it to be.

Interruptions caused by my own experiments, bumping into people I knew or some other unforeseen scenario caused by being 'out' was becoming frustrating, on top of dealing with English inefficiencies.

The home office I had set up worked well in a pinch, but to this day I find working at home *when the kids are home* to be nearly impossible. While I love them to bits and enjoy hearing them having fun, it's not an environment that can support stretches of focused productivity.

With me continually pushing the boundaries of nomadic working, lower-than-expected productivity affected our income, and with a new baby to care for, money was no longer about whether we could afford a family 'holiday' or new iPhone, but about being able to pay the mortgage and put food on the table.

My list began to overwhelm me. I started asking around about a spare desk space, visiting co-working offices and trying once again to work from home.

A friend had a spare desk at his company's office and offered it to me for free, or until he needed it. I drove there each morning, worked at the desk during the day only going out for lunch breaks, and driving back home at night. Being bound to a desk again left me feeling depressed and defeated; reminding me of how I craved my freedom years ago.

With productivity only slightly up, I asked myself whether it was worth the sacrifice of the freedom and inspiration I had become accustomed to by foregoing the office in the first place. The answer was easy—it was *no*, and I determined to get more creative about the problem.

After a week, I thanked my friend and called it quits. I thought maybe if I could create *my own* workspace, I wouldn't have to give up inspiration or work in a typical office environment.

I began looking for a small, private room that was not inside someone else's office, but which I could call my own. After looking online, I called on four different advertisements and arranged viewings at two of them. They were separate rooms within office buildings.

I went home that night to join Ruth in discussing whether or not we could afford rent for a dedicated office, and we concluded that *maybe we could if it was cheap enough.*

The next day I met with the office manager at a building in an ideal location in central Bristol. On the phone he had quoted me a price that was at the very high end of what we might be able to afford.

I was shown through the tiny unit as he informed me of the

additional costs for electricity, phone, internet and a 'maintenance fee' which oddly did not cover anything within my particular unit, but which did manage to drive the monthly cost so far outside of our budget that I politely thanked him for his time and left feeling cynical about the entire situation.

I canceled my other appointment for the following day with the knowledge that *we really couldn't afford it anyway* and sat at the nearest café deep in thought. I knew that working from the little home-office in our dining room wasn't a long-term solution, but it provided a temporary option that *kinda* worked.

My all-or-nothing personality made it hard for me to see options that weren't exactly perfect. Feeling defeated, I took a sip of coffee and grabbed my notebook from my bag and began flipping through page-by-page of incomplete and all-too-familiar tasks until I reached the last page; my #wins page.

RESTARTING

The list of #wins by that time had nearly used up an entire page, and I had several completed notebooks at home with their own full #wins pages. Some items were small #wins, and a few were big #wins. I recalled each time I ticked-off a page and noted its title in the back.

I remembered the trials of getting into cycling and that first time my legs burned up to Abbot's Leigh. I remembered the trip to Florac and ticking off the *Car* page when I first returned home with our Subaru. I remembered that crappy jacket from The North Face I wasted £85 on, and how I eventually ticked off my *rain jacket* page.

All these showed up on my #wins page like a wall of Olympic gold medals.

When I got back home I pulled out my other completed notebooks. I read each #win page and some of the pages where I worked through issues. It was amazing to me how far I'd come.

I had overcome so many obstacles. I had enjoyed so many incredible experiences. I had been swimming in the river of inspiration for years now, and I realized that it was no longer a simple matter of choosing to stop. Rather, it's what I imagine it might feel like to ask Lance Armstrong to stop cycling. Nomadic working had already become a core aspect of who I was as a human... I wasn't just 'trying something out', I had been *living it* for years.

Considering my recent experiences back in an office environment with my friend or on contracts, it all-of-a-sudden dawned on me.

What I'm doing is a thing. It's my thing. It's what works for me. It's the source of my inspiration for much of life—not just work. To stop exploring would be to stop the flow of adventure and inspiration. I can't stop now. This is who I am, it's what I do, and there's no way I'm alone in this.

Now, LET'S DO THIS.

During what became our last couple years in England, I became more purposeful than ever. I went through notebooks like they were going out of style. I tackled every page with an insatiable desire.

The point at which I recognized that *I'm consciously doing this as its own 'thing'* is about when I began to really settle into the lifestyle of it, and looking back, that's the only thing I wish I would have done differently; I wish I would have recognized sooner that *I was doing something different, and that's okay. It's okay to 'own' it.*

I never thought about nomadic working in the same way. For this remaining time in Bristol I finally embraced the different-ness of what I was doing. I accepted it as more than just *not being able to afford an office,* but as a part of who I was. For better or worse, it's something that defines who I am.

I am addicted to inspiration and exploration. I'm addicted to problem-solving and experimentation. But more so, I'm addicted to the richness that nomadic working has brought to my increasingly *whole* life.

CALIFORNIA
CALLING

Our home at Number 7 was plenty big enough for the three of us. Ruth and I shared the master bedroom overlooking Dalrymple Road from the second floor, and Titus occupied his room behind ours with a view of the back garden.

In Bristol, we had an incredible social network of friends and family. Our jobs were satisfying and enjoyable. We were setup very well in most respects, and we knew it. But the better our circumstances became, the more apparent was the problem of our location.

Our home in the borough of St Paul's was situated very close to the city center of Bristol, which offered a lot of conveniences, like being close to food, shopping and transportation.

It was also the illegal drug-center of the city (with a couple related *national* titles, too), and the city's haven for those "on the dole" and a place many homeless called home. To top it off, a brothel had just opened a few doors up from us, and we were starting to see the effects of it.

The City had been providing government housing to those on the dole in St. Paul's for two decades, which meant a noticeable concentration of zero-income families. While the rich cultures of Jamaica, Poland, Pakistan and India were lovely and amazing, they coalesced here in the worst way. We loved the people, but the drugs, crime and subsequent police activity was more active than I'd ever seen when I lived in East LA.

Our neighbors always sat on their porches across the narrow street, smoking weed, arguing or playing guitar. Sometimes they sat on the wall that was two feet from our front window to smoke weed.

I once asked our 70-year-old Jamaican neighbor Johnny why he sat at our house to smoke his 'spliff', and he said it was *because the sun was on our side of the road at this time of day.* Fair enough I guess. I really liked Johnny, but he didn't care about how his behavior was affecting our lives, and neither did any of our other neighbors.

I could often look out my window and witness drug purchases, usage or prostitution from our bedroom and living room windows. The small park across the road was littered with used needles, joint butts, condoms and other unsavory things.

We witnessed police drug raids, brothel raids, fights in the street, naked and distraught prostitutes arguing with their 'coordinators'. Seeing drug sales was the most common occurrence.

It was never really safe to walk through our neighborhood after dark, and this had affected our daily lives since I had set foot in England. If one of us was out after dark, the other worried. It was a circumstance that really bothered me because it was terribly inconvenient to have Ruth worrying about me at night, and if she went out after dark we always arranged company.

In early August of 2011, a riot broke out in our neighborhood just one street away, spilling violence and chaos into our lives for almost 2 days straight. For me, it was the final straw. I wasn't willing to raise our child here.

That Spring we took a long weekend in Cornwall on the south coast of England with the Subaru packed with a young baby boy and some food. While there, we took a few coastal walks in-between discussions of what we could do.

With the issue so deeply on my heart, I mentioned the impossible. *"Maybe we should move to The States."*

I knew the vast implications of such a suggestion—after all, I myself had completely rebuilt my life here in England, and it dawned on me that these were some of the most 'defining' years of my life, from the ages of 24-31.

We would both be leaving our friends and family. We would be leaving the jobs we had painstakingly invested into for the last 6 years, and which we both dearly loved. We refocused our discussions around this idea; exploring every option, possibility and implication.

I described more to Ruth about how things worked in California, and how things "were just easier" there. I talked about how the country was setup for a more 'modern' life, with transportation, housing and most other things being more affordable. I assured Ruth that it would open up our options, and that we would still be near 'family', but *my* family.

It was such a difficult decision with so much at stake. We had slightly different perspectives, too. I had an intimate knowledge of what we could gain by such a move, and Ruth did not.

I had built a life around my needs, but it paled in comparison with what Ruth had spent the last 13 years investing into within Bristol. She had so much more to lose than I did, and I knew that. Before making any decisions, though, we had some due-diligence ahead of us.

With Ruth's maternity leave offering only temporary compensation, and the nature of my business being that monthly income was irregular, there was no way we could take on a larger mortgage in a more desirable area of Bristol.

There were only a couple other areas within central Bristol that offered a higher level of safety, and they were so far out of our financial ability that they were quickly ruled out. We had previously looked at houses outside Bristol, but with a kind of solemnity. We didn't want to be outside Bristol. We didn't want to leave our friends, family and lifestyle.

As our conversation explored and narrowed each option, there was really very little choice in the end. Moving to California was the best way to raise our child, and we were willing to give up everything to give Titus the best chance we could.

After our last day of these discussions at the coast, we returned home to Bristol with heavy hearts. We knew we'd made the right decision, but it hurt. We both had ambitions that would have to somehow be translated into an American setting.

Ruth would not return to the jobs she loved, and I would be abandoning a business that had grown steadily into a real job with freedom, control and options. Our dearest friends would be left behind, and Ruth would no longer be around the corner from the most important person in her life; her big sister. It was the most difficult decision we had ever been faced with as a couple and as new parents.

With 75% reticence and 25% *the hope of new possibility,* we made the decision to move to California just days after I had offered the idea… another evidence of our unusually high-tolerance for risk.

CALIFORNIA PREPARATIONS

The following year in Bristol was a blur of raising a child, selling the house and car, living with friends, many sessions of gathering papers for VISA trips in London and Birmingham, and generally planning the move.

From the day we made the decision to the day we boarded the plane was almost a year and a half—that's how long it took for us to satisfy the requirements of the British and American governments so that our relocation could be legal and permanent.

By the time we were done, our three passports would be worth more than £10,000 in flights and other travel, fees, hotels, days off work and more fees in order for me to remain in England and now, for Ruth and Titus to move to America.

Every consulate or embassy trip was its own little nightmare in one way or another. We weathered a few rejections – one for Ruth's green card – and by the time we got a #win we were usually too exhausted or broke to enjoy it.

Traversing the spiderweb of immigration law could never be possible without vast sums of money and patience. We only had hope. Our typical consulate or embassy visit went like this:

Spend the week prior hunting and gathering a specific set of documents. Organize them logically into a presentable binder while we guessed at strategies based on the little information that was supplied. Train or plane to London, Birmingham or Los Angeles.

Upon arrival, wait in a sterile white lobby with fiberglass chairs arranged in rows facing a dirty white wall in a room speckled with angry people and their screaming children. Wait there for an hour or two. (One time I was forced to wait outside the building for some reason of international law.)

Approach the teller behind their bullet-proof glass window where our greetings are ignored and a hand extended for our documentation. Without eye-contact, they asked our purpose and ignored offers for additional information. Teller leaves their window without a word to some unknown place, carrying our documents and passports.

Upon returning they either give further instructions to wait for a confirmation, or send us away with a scold about how we had not read Paragraph Z of Section X. Maybe next time.

After the bureaucracy we had finally reached a waiting period. Things were appropriately in-motion and we had just sold our house. Problem was, we wouldn't actually be moving to California for several months as we awaited Ruth's Green Card and Titus' US Passport.

We realized there was no reason not to just go out there for (technically) a 'visit' to get a little head-start. We booked a holiday rental in Huntington Beach just a few blocks from the ocean, packed some bags and left.

Upon arrival we met arrangements to buy a car from a seller who would meet us at the airport. We collected the Audi and drove to our holiday rental. We spent a truly lovely 3 months there in Huntington Beach—taking walks on the beach, seeing the local sights and visiting my side of the family.

We bought a 'beach cruiser' bicycle with a kiddie trailer for Ruth and Titus to get around, and I continued my work.

One of the great things about my own work is that 99% of the time, it doesn't matter where I am. Half my British clients didn't even know I was gone, and I was starting work for some Californian clients at the same time.

We cherished those relaxing 3 months in Huntington Beach after we returned to England to make our final preparations for the official move. We spent our last few months back in Bristol seeing friends and packing everything up once more.

It was hard for us both to be actually saying 'goodbye', but deep down we knew it was the right decision. England would always be an important part of our lives.

A NEW
BEGINNING

We boarded the plane on our way to LAX again, with our things in a shipping container somewhere ahead of us at sea. We moved into our small rental home a quarter-mile from the ocean at Huntington Beach—barely 2 blocks from the holiday rental we'd just left. For me personally, I was back in the place that turned the direction of my life 12 years earlier.

Ruth remained a full-time stay-at-home mom while writing on spiritual topics. Our daughter Penny was born in Orange County in July of 2013. I sold that beastly Audi and bought an old Range Rover 'Classic' and commenced the 10-month repair job before she began showing any semblance of reliability.

I worked with a friend who had started an agency while we were friends in California ten years earlier. I enjoyed getting to make some great new friends through that job, and our relationship gave me the flexibility I needed for nomadic working.

Living near the beach was peaceful, but these 2 years in California felt like a 'ramping-up' toward something bigger. We were making a lot of good practical progress, but all that meant our passions were put on-hold for our entire stay in Huntington.

After two years in California we moved to Fort Collins, Colorado, and the fun began. We had been wanting to 'settle down', but until now had not found the right location. We fell in love with Fort Collins after visiting in the winter of 2013. Ruth finally earned her driver's license and started driving.

Northern Colorado has a similar magic to England—every direction you turn looks like a still from *Lord of the Rings* or something. It's just so wild and beautiful. We feel like we have a lot of breathing room here, and the air feels ripe with opportunity.

There's a new chapter ahead of us. My own journey of becoming a nomadic worker isn't over, because now there's a whole new wilderness to explore. I know that for me, nomadic working will evolve alongside the different needs of my new environment, as it always has.

You and I both know what lies ahead; *an adventurous and whole life of creative inspiration.* I wish you even better as we blaze this trail together.

With love,
Chris Lorensson